THE RISE AND FALL OF ZIGGY STARDUST
AND THE SPIDERS FROM MARS

DAVID BOWIE

CLASSIC **ROCK** *ALBUMS*

Series Editor: Clinton Heylin

THE RISE AND FALL OF ZIGGY STARDUST AND THE SPIDERS FROM MARS

DAVID BOWIE

Mark Paytress

SCHIRMER BOOKS
An Imprint of Simon & Schuster Macmillan
New York

Prentice Hall International
London   Mexico City   New Delhi   Singapore   Sydney   Toronto

Schirmer Books
An Imprint of Simon & Schuster Macmillan
1633 Broadway
New York, NY 10019

Library of Congress Catalog Card Number: 97–29053

Printed in the United States of America

Printing Number
10 9 8 7 6 5 4 3 2 1

Library of Congress Cataloging-in-Publication Data

Paytress, Mark.
   The rise and fall of Ziggy Stardust and the Spiders from Mars : David Bowie / Mark Paytress.
      p. cm. — (Classic rock albums)
   Discography: p.
   Includes bibliographical references.
   ISBN 0–02–864771–8 (alk. paper)
   1. Bowie, David. Rise and fall of Ziggy Stardust and the Spiders from Mars. 2. Rock music—1971–1980—History and criticism.
I. Title. II. Series.
ML420.B754P39 1998
782.42166'092—dc21   97–29053
                                                                                  CIP
                                                                                  MN

This paper meets the requirements of ANSI/NISO Z.39.48–1992 (Permanence of Paper).

CONTENTS

ACKNOWLEDGMENTS

My thanks to Peter Doggett, my colleague and editor of many years, for casting an eye over the script. Also for his knowledge, patience, and humor, not forgetting his irreverent lampooning of those we've made it our business to write about (he does a great "Bowie," by the way).

To Keith Badman, Dr. David Buckley, Laurence Hallam, Trevor King, Cliff McLenehan, Carlton Sandercock, Kevin Cann, Mark Adams, Pete Smith, David Wells, and Steve Pafford (of the *Crankin' Out!* Bowie-zine, P.O. Box 3268, London NW6 4NH, U.K.), all of whom helped out with source materials and information.

To John Harrison, whom I encountered far too late in the day, but who nevertheless whizzed through the script with his well-trained eye for Bowie minutiae and furnished several important missing links.

To Ken Scott, my fly on the wall at the *Ziggy* sessions.

To Tony Visconti, Kevin Howlett, and Rick Wakeman, for previous discussions of Bowie's work.

To Clinton Heylin for opening the door, and for excising several howlers, curbing some foolish flights of fancy, and making many helpful suggestions while editing the book.

To my colleagues Andy Davis, Pat Gilbert, and John Reed, for many heated and humorous debating sessions over a quick beer or five.

And to Erika, Norman, Julie-Anne and Chris, Dave, Simon, Vanessa and Mike, for the decades, and to Fiona B, who continues to fill our flat with photos of poodles with Jackie Kennedy hairstyles and other life-enriching objets d'art.

I'd also like to extend a firm and professional handshake to Martin Denny, the late Les Baxter, Burt Bacharach, the Three Suns, Perrey and Kingsley, Andy Williams, the Tony Hatch Orchestra, Francis Lai, and those other barons of Beautiful Music whose work kept my spirits high well into the night while writing this book. And to Captain Beefheart and his Magic Band for making the ultimate rock album, *Trout Mask Replica.*

ZIGGY STARDUST: AN INTRODUCTION

THE SEVENTIES FOR ME STARTED THE TWENTY-FIRST CENTURY. IT HAD SUCH A LOT TO DO WITH BREAKING ABSOLUTES DOWN.

—David Bowie, *An Earthling at 50*

(TV documentary), January 1997

The Rise and Fall of Ziggy Stardust and the Spiders from Mars: a classic album? Well, maybe. In terms of songwriting craft, you'd be hard pressed not to favor several of the cuts on *Hunky Dory;* for originality, *Station to Station* and *Low* are difficult to beat; for sheer avant-pop hedonism, the run of singles with which he bowed out of the seventies represents another high in a career of peaks and a few notable commercial and creative troughs.

Putting the finishing touches on this book, I've been gorging on the advance tape of *Earthling,* which, if you ignore the hyperbole about its being a drum 'n' bass album (three tracks at most), is still a startling (and frankly unexpected) delight, one of the most invigorating returns to form by a major pop artist in recent years. It is virtually impossible to listen to a new album by any long-in-the-tooth performer without greeting it as yet another unloved coda to a once flawless canon. Remarkably, *Earthling* stands up without any of that well-he-was-good-once baggage. (All the

David Bowie performing as
Ziggy Stardust with the
Spiders from Mars at Radio
City Music Hall in New York
City on February 14, 1973
DAGMAR, COURTESY OF
STAR FILE

more shocking because I'd sworn I'd never have any post–*Scary Monsters*
Bowie record in the house.)

So perhaps Bowie has rewritten the book once more. For, ultimately, that is what Bowie has always sought to do. If the *Ziggy Stardust* LP no
longer sounds like the complete musical event it is often held up to be,
that is perhaps because while avoiding the lows that can afflict later Bowie
artifacts, it contains too few lasting moments of sonic exuberance. Yet it
remains a milestone from which rock culture has never really recovered.
Taken in its widest sense, Ziggy—the album, the concept, the live show,
the predominant sense of artifice—generated a set of ideas around which
an entirely new rock aesthetic would be based.

On a musical level, the album popularized hitherto largely untapped
notions of pastiche (Frank Zappa had excelled at this, though his audience was strictly underground). *Ziggy Stardust* was released in 1972, at
a time when rock was firmly in the grip of "progressiveness," a forward-
moving march toward a lofty, neoclassical status, presenting itself in ever

THE RISE AND FALL OF ZIGGY STARDUST AND
THE SPIDERS FROM MARS

more technically adept ways. The record arrived in the midst of an era when rock musicians were happy to dress in jeans and a T-shirt, parading a hirsute if mundane machismo that offered little threat to the parent culture. Bowie's Ziggy escapade moved in the opposite direction, bursting into life dressed in pop's central referents—spunky, three-minute musical epics; sex laced with a frisson of deviance, strangeness, and, lest we forget, fun.

These fundamentals were given a new twist by tapping into another oft-overlooked musical tradition, tucked away in the most unloved corners of American rock. In prying open the window behind which the Velvet Underground lurked and Iggy Pop radiated a bloodcurdling glow, *Ziggy Stardust* was responsible for a dramatic shift in how rock was perceived. The twenty-minute drum solo, the search for roots in archaic folk or country forms, the soothing of the post-psychedelic psyche with gentle songs of introspective depth could now legitimately be discarded in favor of a distinctly playful attitude toward rock and pop's own past. The forward march, having reached a crossroads at the start of the decade, was now thrown into terminal confusion. In its place, pop history was massaged back to life, a scrapbook of source material to be used or discarded on a whim. Four years after *Ziggy,* punk applied the same aesthetic, with far greater consequences. And more recently, the technical facility of sampling, coupled with the launch of the CD, has made rock grave-robbing the predominant contemporary stylistic form. As we remember the past, we are condemned to repeat it in ever more baffling hybrids.

Though the ideas inscribed on the music of *Ziggy Stardust* have had an irreducible effect on how we perceive pop, the record's status as a classic is not based merely on its ramifications for future musical developments. *Ziggy Stardust* the album was just one part of a scheme infinitely more grand than the arrival of a new rock 'n' roll record, to be either ignored or drooled over. The presentation of Bowie the star, the unforgettable sense of theater that dominated the Ziggy shows during 1972 and 1973, and the mantle of hero construction that enveloped the records, the marketing, and the concerts invest *Ziggy Stardust* with meanings that reach far beyond traditional notions of what makes an LP a "classic."

If, with its aura of rock revivalism, *Ziggy Stardust* helped puncture the self-importance that had blighted rock ever since its "recovery" from the perceived excesses of psychedelia, that was only part of the story.

With the album's visual and conceptual innovations, Bowie took rock to new heights of complexity—which is why he is sometimes regarded as one of the most pretentious men working in the medium. With his eyebrows in perpetual Arc de Triomphe mode, he has been widely credited as being the person most responsible for placing proverbial quotation marks around every activity, a thoroughly postmodern man whose work continually effaces the idea of a unique and all-knowing self. Like Bob Dylan, he has done this by projecting a multiplicity of artistic shifts. Unlike Dylan's, these are designed to create the impression of someone working at the behest of the micronarrative of contemporary fashion, rather than maintaining the apparent dignity of creative (dis)continuity.

And that's precisely where Bowie's true importance lies. Eschewing the idea that he's the unflappable center of a creative world, his version of modern man is fractured and spongelike, rather than having a capacity to withstand the ebb and flow of cultural change. In this respect, his work is more in keeping with contemporary sensibilities than the romantic notion of a fortresslike self (popular in late sixties rock), a legacy of Enlightenment notions of identity. That's why he found Andy Warhol—the man who personified the denial of human essence—so fascinating, and why he was able to invest in the Ziggy doppelganger something that held far greater significance than the simple exchange of one costume for another.

For Bowie, life has been his stage: The series of guises that has sustained him since the late sixties exteriorized his suspicion that at the heart of his inner self is an emptiness to be enriched by whatever takes his fancy. By donning the alter ego of Ziggy and articulating the absence that lay at the heart of his fragmented self, he helped elevate the quest for self-knowledge, simultaneously reinforcing and demystifying the notion of stardom in the process.

In this book, I explore the unfolding of this oeuvre, which culminated so spectacularly in the Ziggy project. Rather than simply chronicle the minutiae of events that catapulted him to stardom during 1972 and 1973 (recounted many times before), I have chosen to take the long view, seeking to fix *Ziggy Stardust* in its wider context. This might not satisfy the seemingly unquenchable thirst for tales of rock 'n' roll debauchery, or the fact collectors hoping for scraps of evidence confirming yet another long-lost *Ziggy* outtake. Those details seem somehow out of place here, shedding little light on why *The Rise and Fall of Ziggy Stardust and the Spiders from Mars* should be so highly regarded.

When I listen to the album now, as a late thirtysomething, my instinct is still to succumb uncritically to its charms. That's how I enjoyed pop music as a child of the sixties, and for all the subsequent struggles to eke out reasons why certain records (and the stars behind them) tickled my psyche, the tendency to lose my head and revel in their primeval pleasures hasn't entirely waned with age. That said, twenty-five years after *Ziggy Stardust,* my intention is to provide a more reflective view, one that at least addresses the pull toward some kind of understanding. After all, it is one of the most important records in forty years of pop history; we ought to know why.

More than any predecessor, *Ziggy Stardust* is a deliberately self-contained work, a concept album by a rock group passing itself off as an archetypal rock group, which toured the world for a year before the masks were fully revealed. The stakes were high: How easily it could have ended in disaster, an unashamed stab at wish fulfillment greeted by a stultifying silence. But the scale of its success, coupled with the reaction of its detractors, had a cataclysmic effect, and the many debates prompted by the audacious escapade (quite likely the first of its kind on such a scale) epitomized the crisis then facing popular music. There can be little doubt that *Ziggy Stardust* helped revolutionize many aspects of the medium. It wasn't that rock music never sounded quite the same again; more that rock culture pre-Ziggy always seemed much more quaint in its wake. Whether that's a good or a bad thing is for you to decide.

THE RISE AND FALL OF ZIGGY STARDUST
AND THE SPIDERS FROM MARS

DAVID BOWIE

David Bowie is Ziggy Stardust live at the Rainbow

Sat. August 19
Sun. August 20

SOLD OUT

David Bowie will be appearing at:

Locarno Bristol	Aug 27
Starkers Bournemouth	Aug 31
Top Rank Doncaster	Sept 1
Hard Rock Manchester	Sept 2
Hard Rock Manchester	Sept 3
Top Rank Liverpool	Sept 4
Top Rank Sunderland	Sept 5
Top Rank Sheffield	Sept 6
Top Rank Hanley-Stoke on Trent	Sept 7

RISE AND FALL OF ZIGGY STARDUST

BIRTHING THE TRIPTYCH, OR HOW I LEARNED TO LOVE THE OTHER

I COULD MAKE IT ALL WORTHWHILE
AS A ROCK 'N' ROLL STAR.

—"Star," from *The Rise and
Fall of Ziggy Stardust and the Spiders from Mars*

THE ONE QUALITY THEY ALL SHARED WAS
THEIR REMOTENESS, A MENTAL AND PHYSICAL INAC-
CESSIBILITY WHICH MANIFESTED ITSELF IN THE
PURCHASING OF WHITE ROLLS-ROYCES AND LIGHT-
WEIGHT LAMBORGHINIS. THEY GAVE THE AUDIENCE
SOMETHING TO LOOK UP AT AGAIN.

—*Melody Maker*, 1 January 1972,
welcoming the return of the glam rock idol

AND I'M GONNA MAKE MY DREAM
TELL THEM I WILL LIVE MY DREAM.

—"When I Live My Dream," 1967

1

David Bowie today might be characterized as the most polished, professional ex–basket case in pop. A profound change in direction (musical, sartorial, and presumably psychological) through the eighties has had critics and longtime admirers reading last rites. Many explanations have poured forth—the apparently drug-free Mr. B had severed the ties with his muse; then well into his thirties, age had tempered his desire to flirt with the unknown; his rich and contented lifestyle was part of a Faustian pact that compelled him to surrender his imagination; his bid to become a respectable member of the jet set was the inevitable resting point for a career that, from the beginning, had shown an almost unhealthy obsession with celebrity.

When *The Rise and Fall of Ziggy Stardust and the Spiders from Mars* was first released in June 1972, David Bowie was riding the tide of six months of media hype in the pages of the British music press, prompted by a declaration to Michael Watts in *Melody Maker* that he was gay, or at the very least bisexual. In the light of that attention, prompted by the fact that homosexuality in pop was still latent rather than overt, his concerts, which were still being held in unexceptional provincial halls around Britain, buzzed with a peculiar feeling that something Genuinely Important was unfolding before the audience's eyes.

"I'm going to be huge, and it's quite frightening in a way," Bowie told Watts in that infamous interview, probably the most important he would ever give. There were good reasons for his presumptuousness, not least that the conditions for the arrival of an intelligent, musically inspired, and experienced artist with feet in both the rock and pop camps were perfect. And he had a support system and well-oiled hype machine behind him. At least as revealing was the way he sought to qualify his comment: that the magnification of self he'd been searching for, from the moment he'd begun grooming and dyeing his hair at school to become the class peacock, was something to be feared.

If the "I'm Gay" cover story at the start of 1972 was Bowie's launching pad, his moment of truth when all eyes were fixed onto the do-or-die trajectory of his stardom-seeking mission, it had been years in the making, the end product of countless tests and experiments, of aborted dry runs and occasional breakthroughs. Able at last to detach himself from the indignity of past failures, he could now offer to the world a précis of his own prior investigations and preoccupations through the guise of a new, all-embracing alter ego. In making himself a tabula rasa, he was forced to confront the traumas of rebirth. In January 1972, when he had yet to step fully into character, Bowie expressed fear precisely because his own easily detectable fingerprint was still on the button. Only during the summer, when Ziggy was brought properly into play, could Bowie fully revel in the estrangement of a doppelganger, cutting himself free from the desperation of his earlier life, or, more accurately, lives.

Although Ziggy was the most famous of several alter egos that helped sustain interest in Bowie through the seventies, those character projections were grounded in something quite different from the simple exchange of stylistic hats he'd worn during the previous decade. His inventory of previous guises read like a virtual genealogy of British youth subcultures: a John Lee Hooker–fixated suburban bluesman; a beatnik-inspired spokesman for the International League for the Preservation of Animal Filament (a pro-longhaired-men pressure group); a lacquer-headed and sharply suited Mod; a serious and rather subdued songwriter with wide-ranging showman ambitions; a pancake-faced artist in mime; a hippie mystic with delusions of transforming the world into one giant Arts Laboratory; and a curly haired, acoustic guitar–toting Bob Dylan figure. His *The Man Who Sold the World* venture was the first to utilize the guise of alter ego in more oppositional ways, though without a fully developed body of ideas to support it, nor the ability to transform the persona into a living theatrical device, it was less a dry run for *Ziggy Stardust* than a bridge toward that ultimate realization.

Unlike Ziggy and the parade of characters that followed (Aladdin Sane, Halloween Jack, Plastic Soul man, the Thin White Duke), this roll call of stylistic shifts was not intrinsic to the aesthetic with which Bowie would redraw the boundaries between image construction and rock music. Instead, these earlier transformations can be seen as natural progressions, propelled as much by the culture(s) he found himself in as by his own auteurist "grasshopper" instincts. During the sixties, both the sound and the vision of pop had altered dramatically, developments that were a by-product of the fast turnover of fashions in the quest for settling on an "authentic" identity—an authenticity that Bowie was later to refute.

For Bowie, this process was partly an attempt to keep up with the Joneses, partly inspired by his need to run away from them, and sometimes an attempt to break with type and design a life for himself in opposition to contemporary currents. The unifying factor was a will to "be somebody," to fulfill the dream he had memorably declared to anyone who was listening on his last day in school. Armed with two O-levels—one for art—he bade farewell with the words "I want to be a pop idol."

It is impossible to understand the genesis, the execution, or the watershed effects of *Ziggy Stardust* without paying attention to the centrality of pop stardom in Bowie's early life. There are plenty of formal biographies that describe his early years in more detail than is necessary. I do not intend to compete with them. But a judicious sifting through the complex path that led him to *Ziggy Stardust* is an essential part of my quest.

Bowie's teenage wilderness neatly coincided with the gold-lamé era of vintage rock 'n' roll. Family life in his rather quiet corner of England in Bromley, Kent, was rudely interrupted by an invasion of mainly American hip-swinging, lip-curling singers giving vent to youthful frustrations in a manner that was regarded as crude and even morally threatening. Bowie has never forgotten his rock 'n' roll baptism when, as nine-year-old David Jones, he watched his older cousin Kristina dance with hitherto unseen abandon to Elvis Presley's latest hit record, "Hound Dog." Though oblivious to the undercurrents that probably inflamed the moment (the dark continent of female sexuality aroused into bodily action by the sounds of a man's voice relayed by something as innocuous as a 78-rpm disc), Jones was nevertheless drawn into this alternative world. It was antithetical to the slow-motion existence of his family, who measured their lives out in regular mealtimes and an efficiently functioning household.

Within weeks, young David had his own heroes: the boogie-woogie piano man Fats Domino and that other diamanté shrieker from New Orleans, Little Richard. David Jones probably knew little about the men behind the hits, but the later discovery that both were black Americans, and thus at least doubly removed from his own existence, must have prompted an added layer of excitement, perhaps even a hint of danger. Vive la différance! He had made a crucial discovery.

Suitably enriched by his immersion in the altered states of sound, geography, and color, Jones played out his early teenage life to the music of strangely named men who dressed in the neon brightness of that crucible of Britain's nascent rock 'n' roll subculture, the milk bar. Elvis, Gene, Chuck, Conway, and later messieurs Eager, Wilde, Gentle, and Fury, were all relatively invisible to this pleasure-seeking pubescent, though all were bathed in the incandescent glow of what David Jones was beginning to understand was meant by "stardom."

Ever since the invention of the matinee idol, stars have provided role models for teenagers to emulate. David, with only an errant older step-brother to provide an alternative source of inspiration, took these faraway idols to heart. He was soon attending Bromley Technical College (where he'd been placed in the arts track) dressed in attention-grabbing Chelsea boots, trousers that widened to fourteen inches at the bottom, and narrow ties. His hair was sculpted with care, one style even inspiring a nickname, "Luther." His passion for all things American (and therefore exotic) extended to following such unlikely pursuits as baseball and American football. Daring to be different, he discovered, was a form of stardom; his final school report, which described him as "a complete exhibitionist," indicated that he was successful in his endeavors.

David Jones's first taste of musical exhibitionism took place on a Scouts' camping trip in August 1958. He was eleven years old and per-formed two Lonnie Donegan songs, skiffle music that was still standard currency in fifties pop's slow-changing lexicon of styles. His first serious venture was playing sax and occasionally singing with a local band, the Konrads, in 1963. It is just possible that both the band's name and Jones's newly blond hair were inspired by Jess Conrad, a Joe Meek protégé and pre-Beatles would-be pop icon, a peroxide-rinsed and alto-gether more campy variant of the late-fifties American rockers. This assessment is not spurious: Jones's band once backed the star, sometime before settling on the Konrads name.

The story of the Jones boy who would become Bowie is littered with the borrowed debris of his peers and contemporaries, a patchwork of iconic references that would ignite many years later, after he'd loaded them onto the distended star of his own making, Ziggy Stardust. But he did stick his neck out once before, in November 1964, at the behest of his manager, Leslie Conn, who'd set him up as a spokesman for long-haired youths. This publicity stunt, which won him (then sporting extend-ed Keith Relf tresses) coverage on television and in the national press, was a salutary exercise in how a gimmick could engage the public before being forgotten as quickly as morning came.

When the Beatles exploded onto the international stage during 1963 and 1964, David Jones, like many aspiring young musicians, must have sensed that his time had come. Siding with the rougher R&B acts of suburban London, such as the Pretty Things, the Yardbirds, and above all the Rolling Stones, he quit the Konrads and teamed up with the King Bees, who'd taken their name from Slim Harpo's "I'm a King Bee," a staple of the Stones' live act. If the King Bees' deal with Decca in the spring of 1964 gave him the impression that pop idolatry was just around the corner, he was mistaken: The impact of the King Bees' lone 45, "Liza Jane," made singing frontman David Jones a star among his friends and family, but a nobody to the world at large. It was a desperate cycle he was to repeat time and again.

For the next couple of years, Jones persevered with groups, not because he was happy to share the acclaim (should there have been any to spare) with his supporting instrumentalists, but for the simple reason that young soloists were distinctly unfashionable, bringing to mind the fates of bygone stars. He said as much in an interview with the fan magazine *Beat '64:* "I would sooner achieve the status as a Manish Boy that Mick Jagger enjoys as a Rolling Stone than end up a small-name solo singer." Nevertheless, by 1966, after spells fronting the Manish Boys and the Lower Third had yielded no commercial breakthrough, Jones—encouraged by the examples of Bob Dylan and Britain's own protesting folkie, Donovan—had seen the future and decided it was a solitary one. (When he recruited his next band, the Buzz, in 1966, it was made clear that they were his backing musicians.)

By the mid-sixties, David Jones had risen as far as the stages of London's club scene, a couple of appearances on television, and a string of records that nobody wanted. Hundreds of other part-time pop dreamers took that as a cue to return to the dimly lit world of office and factory work they'd been primed for. But not fledgling Ziggy. He sat in the La Giaconda coffee bar on Denmark Street, London's equivalent to Tin Pan Alley, bending the ear of anyone likely to succumb to his nascent star quality and offer him a break. He'd stare across the crowded room at the luminaries of Swinging London—Steve Marriott and the Small Faces, the Moody Blues—and the occasional old-school entertainer, such as Kenny Lynch or Anthony Newley, and wonder why fame continued to elude him. It's no surprise to learn that one of the discarded songs from his spell with the Lower Third was titled "I Lost My Confidence."

His January 1966 single (credited to David Bowie and the Lower Third), the self-penned "Can't Help Thinking About Me," neatly summarized his predicament (he later described the song as "an illuminating little piece"). Precisely the hymn to self-absorption that its title suggests, it documents his flight from the obscurity of the family nest ("I'll leave them all in the never-never land") and the difficulties he faced trying to stand on his own feet. His desire for celebrity and his fears about attaining it are revealed: "I'm on my own / I've got a long way to go / I hope I make it on my own." Interestingly, he posits this particular flight of fancy alongside a desire to feel "secure again."

What more fitting reconciliation of his twin hopes than the arrival of a man named Kenneth Pitt, who had this to say of their first encounter: "His burgeoning charisma was undeniable, but I was particularly struck by the artistry with which he used his body, as if it were an accompanying instrument, essential to the singer and the song." For the next four years, Pitt would both protect and nurture David's sense of self, becoming his manager and his number one cheerleader, there to console him as each boost was canceled out by yet another setback.

Months before their first encounter at the Marquee Club in April 1967, Pitt had already left an indelible mark on the career of his future charge. He advised Ralph Horton, then handling David's affairs, that there were already several David Joneses in the entertainment world. These included an American soul singer and an up-and-coming young singing actor from Manchester, then part of Lionel Bart's stage show *Oliver* and soon to be front man for the Monkees; there was also a David John, leader of an R&B combo, the Mood.

The Bromley-raised David Jones, who'd briefly styled himself David Jay back in 1963, saw the adoption of a new stage name as an opportunity to kick start his faltering career. And what better omen than to style himself after Colonel James Bowie, Davy Crockett's sidekick in John Wayne's lengthy historical epic *The Alamo*. Colonel Bowie, played by Richard Widmark, was a hero of the American republic whose name derived from the hunting knife vital to survival in the frontier days. "I wanted a truism about cutting through the lies and all that," was Bowie's belated—and somewhat unlikely—explanation to Beat writer William Burroughs many years later. More like cutting himself adrift from the spectacularly unsuccessful David Jones and having no wish to be mistaken for anyone else.

The relationship between Ken Pitt and the newly christened David Bowie was almost Svengalian. The rarefied tastes of a public school–educated pop manager provided a window to an aesthete's world as alien to David as the fast-moving culture of boom-time America had been to him as a schoolboy. Pitt's central London flat was crammed with exemplary cultural artifacts: Wilde first editions and Beardsley prints, antique furniture, and classically stylish upholstery. Bowie, who moved into Pitt's residence in June 1967, became a willing pupil, grilling his mentor on everything from fin-de-siècle art and culture and the aesthetics of contemporary theater to the golden rules of pop success.

But Pitt would never have tried to mold a star out of nothing for the increasingly sophisticated late sixties market. Bowie's desire to become the Renaissance man of pop had been apparent for some time. The press release that had accompanied "Can't Help Thinking About Me" in early 1966, for example, had trumpeted his aspirations to act and dance, stated that he was writing a musical, and sought to present a picture of an artiste rather than someone who'd only recently shed his rough-and-ready R&B skin. "Gone are the outlandish clothes, the long hair and the wild appearance," it had announced. "Instead we find a quiet, talented vocalist and songwriter."

The campaign that helped relaunch Bowie in 1972, and the one that put an end to years spent drifting aimlessly around the pop cosmos, has often been likened to a neatly planned military coup. And no aspect of *Ziggy Stardust* prehistory lends support to this "stardom at all costs" thesis more than Pitt's projection of Bowie as a multitalented all-rounder. Toward the end of their relationship, on the cusp of the new decade, it would become clear that Bowie's trust in his manager's judgment was dwindling. But in 1967, the idea that David Bowie would be groomed as a new kind of pop star, a sort of Tommy Steele for thinking young adults, showed a recognition that pop was changing fast.

The Bowie-Pitt partnership had read the sands well: 1967 welcomed a marked maturity in pop. Unfortunately, it was largely based on technological advances, such as studio multitracking and a range of new sound capabilities, and on a show of instrumental dexterity, inspired by the extended "blowing" sessions of modern jazz. Both developments met

cide—is no less ludicrous than that of Townshend's *Tommy,* where a deaf, dumb, and blind boy ends up fronting an international spiritual cult. But having been discarded by a fourth record company in as many years, finding someone to back this tried, tested, and endlessly rejected singer with a distinctly novel venture was a vain hope.

These woeful pre–*Ziggy Stardust* attempts to tether himself to the pop gravy train required Bowie to widen the parameters of his work during 1968. Still reeling from his many rejections, he momentarily appeared to retract from the Bowie-as-auteur stance of his debut album, concentrating instead on writing songs for others, chiefly Pitt's other main concern, Scottish beat combo the Beatstalkers. With a view to hitting the cabaret trail, he also compiled a list of standards for his musical sets that included middle-of-the-road crowd pleasers such as "Trains and Boats and Planes" and "Can't Get Used to Losing You" and benign material from the Lennon-McCartney songbook, including "Yellow Submarine," "When I'm 64," and "All You Need Is Love."

Little came of this immersion in the musical identities of others; instead Bowie reemerged with a project more palatable to a growing underground audience. This was Feathers, a mixed-media trio, formed with his new girlfriend Hermione Farthingale and guitarist John "Hutch" Hutchinson, who'd previously been a member of Bowie's 1966 backing band the Buzz. The trio read Beat-inspired poetry and sang a more provocative selection of covers, including Leonard Cohen's "Lady Midnight" and Jacques Brel's "Port of Amsterdam" and "Next." The centerpiece, or at least the most notable feature, was Bowie's performance of a mime-plus-narrative sketch called "The Mask."

The brief life of Feathers climaxed in the shooting of a promotional film funded by Pitt in a bid to reawaken interest in the varied talents of his client. The film, *Love You till Tuesday* (issued on video in 1984), provides a useful snapshot of Pitt's attempt to market Bowie as someone rather more than your average pop singer. Feathers appear infrequently in the thirty-minute short, and when they do, the sweet-sounding three-piece invites comparison with the watered-down antipodean folk-pop trio the Seekers. Elsewhere in the film Bowie hams it up in Tommy Steele fashion for "Love You till Tuesday," gives a *Mary Poppins*–style set-piece performance—complete with straw hat and striped jacket—during "Rubber Band," and physically contorts himself back into childhood for "When I'm

Five." But it is his execution of "The Mask" that—despite its title—is most revealing.

In the sketch, the main character acquires a mask and parades it for the benefit of his parents and workmates. Enjoying the role of entertainer, he progresses to the stage at a local concert, and before long he's signing autographs, making films, and appearing on television. "It had a very strange effect on me, though," says the narrator. Reaching the pinnacle of British stagecraft with a show at the London Palladium, the act ends abruptly when the performer is strangled as he attempts to remove the mask. The newspapers report the tragic death but omit to mention the mask. Was it, like the stardom bestowed upon its holder, merely an illusion? If that's the question Bowie intended, then "The Mask" stands as his first notable investigation of the nature of stardom. The days of uncritically seeking stardom for its own sake were over.

The questioning nature of "The Mask" may well have been a by-product of Bowie's growing immersion in the culture of the underground; a culture that, when it wasn't flat on its collective back dreaming of utopia, encouraged critical thinking about many aspects of society and culture. The closing performance in the film implied that Bowie was not averse at this stage to postulating an Eden on Earth. There was still mileage in his song "When I Live My Dream," and the accompanying footage of the three Feathers enjoying a walk through a rustic idyll nailed the "dream" to a potent contemporary fantasy.

The mysticism of the era also began to rub off on Bowie, as he skillfully harnessed it in yet another installment of his heroic quest. Explaining his interest in Buddhism to writer George Tremlett, he reduced the creed to a desire "to try and make each moment of one's life one of the happiest, and if it is not, try and find out why."

A personal crisis prompted by the surprise departure of Hermione from his life may have motivated Bowie's next move, an attempt to find comfort in the living, breathing scene of an Arts Laboratory. Modeled on Jim Haynes's pioneering mixed-media space on Drury Lane, Bowie's arts lab was located in the back room of the Three Tuns pub in Beckenham. While barely lasting the summer, the Beckenham arts lab won him coverage in the underground press ("I feel compassion as a source of energy, the individual is less important than the source of energy of which he is part," he told *International Times*) and provided him with a regular audience. The venture reached its zenith in August with the free open-air "Growth" festival, later immortalized in his 1969 cut "Memory of a Free Festival."

If the arts lab was designed to satisfy Bowie's many-sided artistic urges, he hadn't lost sight of his real goal. In fact, he'd finally written a song that had everyone around him fired up, not the least Ken Pitt. Pitt's thinking behind the *Love You till Tuesday* film had been to present his charge as a gifted all-rounder, then hit the record company executives with a song they'd find irresistible. That track, dressed up in the film's most elaborate set piece, was "Space Oddity."

Early in 1969, "Space Oddity" featured a minor singing role for Bowie's partner Hutch, but the disbanding of Feathers after Hermione's departure had prompted Bowie to return to a solo career. That spring, while Ken Pitt was busy talking up his boy wonder to any record company that bothered to listen, Bowie fashioned a hip pop-star image loosely based on Bob Dylan. Pitt was less than enamored with Bowie's new hairstyle, which he later described as "a failed Afro," and regarded it as indicative of a growing gulf between them. But for now, his main concern was that he at last had the proof to match his conviction that David Bowie was a success story waiting to happen. The A&R department at Philips/Mercury agreed and signed Bowie to a one-year deal with two further one-year options. This type of deal was standard practice at the time and suggested that the company wanted the song but were hedging their bets as to whether their new signing would be anything more than a one-hit wonder. Producer Tony Visconti, who'd worked with Bowie irregularly since late 1967, thought the move a grave misjudgment. Refusing to become involved in what he felt was a shameless lunge at the commercial market, where he believed Bowie was wasted, Visconti passed the production reins over to Gus Dudgeon.

In a way, Visconti was right. "Space Oddity" was a hit, albeit a slow-moving one that took the best part of three months to find its way onto the charts. But as with another futuristic moon-landing tie-in, Zager and Evans's "In The Year 2525," both the single and its singer quickly faded from view. The tie-in album, again simply titled *David Bowie,* was a flop, as was a prestigious concert appearance at the Purcell Room in London, when the press failed to show at what was meant to be a showcase performance. That autumn, Bowie went on a nationwide tour with the hard-rocking supergroup Humble Pie—which was precisely what Bowie was forced to eat night after night as indignant audiences abused him during his twenty-minute set. Although "Space Oddity" was still riding high, the mime sequence apparently wasn't to their liking.

And Fall . . .

DON'T WANNA STAY ALIVE, WHEN YOU'RE TWENTY-FIVE.

—"All the Young Dudes," written by

David Bowie for Mott the Hoople, 1972

I COULD NEVER TAKE ALL THAT [RICHARD NEVILLE STUFF] SERIOUSLY, BECAUSE AS YOU KNOW, I'M AN AWFUL FATALIST. I KNEW NOTHING WOULD HAPPEN. . . . I'M PESSIMISTIC ABOUT NEW THINGS, NEW PROJECTS, NEW IDEAS, AS FAR AS SOCIETY'S CONCERNED. I THINK IT'S ALL OVER PERSONALLY. I THINK THE END OF THE WORLD HAPPENED TEN YEARS AGO. THIS IS IT.

—Speaking to Charles Shaar Murray,

1974

PLANET EARTH IS BLUE, AND THERE'S NOTHING I CAN DO.

—"Space Oddity," 1969

The brutal hangover from misspent sixties idealism explains why a fragile and solitary singer briefly became a hate figure for the increasingly cynical underground. And David Bowie had the phlegm-festooned satin jacket to prove it. The youth market's brief flirtation with good vibes and sagelike nods of approval for all manner of experimental artistic endeavors was over. Even the Marc Bolan–fronted Tyrannosaurus Rex, the epitome of English antiurban escape into folkloric fields of innocence, had begun to embrace electricity in a bid to meet the bolder, brasher require-ments of rock's newfound muscularity.

Nineteen sixty-nine was the year the bodies began to pile up. The Rolling Stones' Brian Jones was the first, in July of that year. He was fol-lowed a month later by Sharon Tate and her houseguests, who died at the hands of a commune-dwelling hippie gang strung out on paranoia and bad acid. The gun-wielding Meredith Hunter was stabbed to death near the stage at the Rolling Stones' "Woodstock West" festival at Altamont. Then, in 1970, the stars really began to fall: Jimi Hendrix, the first black man in ultrasonic space, refused to rouse from a drug-induced stupor; Canned Heat's Al Wilson pined away under the shade of a giant redwood tree that he feared was endangered by urban development; Janis Joplin found true happiness at the end of a syringe.

These headline deaths complicated the nature of pop stardom, an existence with a self-critical dimension that could be traced a lot further back than Dylan's warning not to "follow leaders" in 1965, was enshrined in cinematic form by the 1967 cult film *Privilege,* and became a virtual industry after the Beatles packed their bags and flew off to the Maharishi's idyll in India (an experience so "real" that Ringo Starr returned home early, complaining that the spiritual retreat was rather like a holiday camp).

"Turn on, tune in, drop out": Timothy Leary's counterculture mantra made literal the connection between drugs, music, and the creation of a new (anti)social order. The glitzy trappings of the old entertainment indus-try were cast aside in favor of "music for the people" rhetoric. Performers dressed down in the Kathmandu-meets-California style they shared with their audiences, creating a new communion that would levitate the Pentagon and cast off similar forces of oppression. And the hearts and minds of the flower children would be free to flourish in a brand-spank-ing-new Age of Aquarius.

This mass séance of self-improvement took its greatest hold in pock-ets where the fires of idealism burned brightest, but the growing popular-ity of underground resistance carried with it the seeds of its own destruc-tion. The keep-'em-coming, package-tour philosophy of pop's earlier days was banished overnight as rock's new grandiose ideologies required over-sized showpieces. And that meant the triumph of the forty-minute LP (which gave the "message" more time to develop) at the expense of the increasingly maligned three-minute 45, and bigger stages, onto which would inevitably step bigger stars.

The so-called heroes of the underground were faced with a painful contradiction. On the one hand, they were messengers from a potentially revolutionary subculture that looked onward, inward, and outward; anywhere that pointed away from the hopelessly repressed adult world, with its value system that was fucking with the minds of its people. Yet they were forced into the uncomfortable rank of demigods: guitar-toting warriors who were expected to lead the "furry freak" uprising, to be the first to tear down the walls. On top of that, they were the front line of a booming industry, product peddlers whose creative freedoms were funded by the corporate dollar.

It's hardly surprising that the responsibility proved too much for some. The literature of the late sixties is rife with allusions to an inability to reconcile these conflicts. The history books continue to record the names of the sacrificed underground heroes with a breathlessness that verges on the fetishistic: Syd Barrett; Eric Burdon; Pigpen; Scott Walker; Skip Spence; Vincent Crane; Jim Morrison; Arthur Lee; Eric Clapton; Steve Peregrine-Took; Brian Wilson; Roky Erickson; John Phillips; Ace Kefford; Peter Green.

To David Bowie, an onlooker rather than a participant in these star-crossed times, this catalog of casualties unable or unwilling to deal with the pressures of contemporary celebrity provided an endless source of fascination. He reveled in the allure of icons and had an acutely personal interest in the effects of life in a pressure cooker. Inevitably, the fractured courses of these "leper messiahs" began to make inroads into his own work, a theme that would culminate in the Ziggy project.

Much, perhaps too much, has been made of the influence of family history on Bowie's work. A theme explored to the hilt in *Alias David Bowie,* Peter and Leni Gillman's thoroughly researched study, it nevertheless occupies a crucial place in the development of Bowie's oeuvre. The unconscious flight from reality that manifests itself in schizophrenia or depression had, as the Gillmans point out, affected Bowie's family deeply. While keener to downplay this element in recent years (when the Gillmans' book was serialized in the *Sunday Times* in 1985, Bowie's office was moved to reject suggestions about the link between the "content of his work and the traumas that have afflicted his family and especially his half brother Terry"), the singer has clearly made these links himself. "Well, my family's nuts," he once said, adding, "There's quite an amount of insanity within any family. I think we've just got more than our fair share."

While at least three aunts had been diagnosed as suffering from mental illness (most commonly schizophrenia), Bowie's single most important confrontation with mental illness was that experienced by his half-brother, Terry Burns. Ten years his senior, Terry was only an intermittent visitor to David's circle of existence, although that did not diminish his influence. On the contrary, as Bowie said as recently as 1993, "I saw so little of him and I think I unconsciously exaggerated his importance. I invented this hero-worship to discharge my guilt and failure, and to set myself free from my own hang-ups."

While young David Jones enjoyed a fairly charmed home life with his parents John Jones and Peggy Burns, Terry, Peggy's child by another liaison, was the outsider who endured a distressing relationship with David's father. When the family left Brixton for Bromley during the winter of 1952–53, Terry was left behind to fend for himself, although after taking a swipe at a landlord in one of his increasingly recurrent mood swings, he was reluctantly accepted back into the family nest and given the smallest room in the house. A National Service call-up in 1955 was his opportunity to flee his dysfunctional environment, and, for the next three years, he was posted with the Royal Air Force, first in Malta, then in Libya. He returned in February 1958 to discover that his tiny room had disappeared, knocked through to give David more generous living space.

Banished from the family home for good, Terry nevertheless maintained a close affection for David, by now passionate about rock 'n' roll and curious about the rituals of male adulthood. Terry introduced his doting half-sibling to the coffee bars of the West End, discussions of jazz music, and Beat writers Jack Kerouac and William Burroughs, opening up a barely understood but intriguing new world for the aspiring escapee.

By 1965, when evidence of Terry's mental illness began to reach the family, David, now eighteen, was already aware of the close proximity between art and madness in the popular imagination. The notion of the romantic artist, someone gifted with the ability to observe the world from a peculiar vantage point, as if on the outskirts of civilization, was a cornerstone of the bourgeois aesthetic. In the words of the nineteenth-century French poet Arthur Rimbaud: "The poet makes himself a seer by a long, prodigious and rational disordering of the senses. . . . He reaches [for] the unknown and even if, crazed, he ends up by losing the understanding of his visions, at least he has seen them."

The sense of this godlike status, bestowed as much to bolster the facade of a "free world" capable of tolerating its eccentrics as a genuine recognition of an artist's worth, was often colored by tales pertaining to a life lived at the creative edge. Stories such as that of Salvador Dali smearing himself in excrement in a bid to woo his future wife (he was successful), or Mozart fainting when he heard a wrong note played at a performance of one of his symphonies, were manna from heaven for impressionable young thrill seekers such as David Jones. But there was one significant lesson to understand: While the clinically mad are generally feared, the creatively "mad" often end up revered.

David Jones's own idols, who operated in the little-esteemed culture of pop, were routinely pilloried in the press with language usually reserved for inmates of asylums. Jerry Lee was insane, Elvis mentally disturbed— even their audiences were apparently hypnotized by a kind of collective madness. Rock 'n' rollers, like the fine artists and writers of high culture, were capable of expressing the *dérèglement de tous sens* that, as the Jones family history amply showed, could burst through the veneer of normality at any given moment. Such eruptions, be they individual psychological disorders of the kind that afflicted Terry or collective expressions such as the hysteria that surrounded rock 'n' roll, were the ultimate badges of difference, perfect flights of fancy from soulless suburbia into the acute emotional fragility of the Other.

But Bowie was already too engrossed in his own creative endeavours to let the news of Terry's "fall" overly taint his perception of stardom and the artistic outsider. In fact, this news was likely to have had the opposite effect: Terry's increasingly erratic behavior was apparent proof of a strong familial urge to exist beyond the strict confines of ordinary life.

Bowie's response to his sense of disorientation and disintegration on the one hand, and his seemingly incompatible "will to power" on the other, was to bypass the crisis by dissolving his "authentic" self, replacing it with a series of guises under which he could successfully play the star. Disintegration lay at the heart of his work, not only in the sense of his own erased subjectivity, but in his understanding of the world at large.

In an interview with *New Musical Express* around the time of the release of the *Ziggy Stardust* LP, Bowie told Andrew Tyler: "People like Lou [Reed] and I are probably predicting the end of an era, and I mean that catastrophically. Any society that allows people like Lou and I to become rampant is pretty well lost." Bowie's alienation wasn't merely from himself, but from a world that he could neither control nor understand. The madness he saw in the eyes of his brother was only one part of the equation. At least as frightening were the visions of dystopia that increasingly colored his own outlook: the banality of evil that could strike so deeply into the heart of so-called civilized culture that six million innocents could be wiped out in death factories; that could create a mushroom-shaped threat capable of wiping out the world at the press of a button; that tolerated exorbitant levels of violence and corruption in society. He suspected that evil was the foundation that lay beneath the spectacle of shiny consumer durables and escapist light entertainment.

Terry's descent into a personal hell was mirrored everywhere by the world in which Bowie found himself, a world where even pop records were beginning to bring more weighty concerns to an entertainment industry dominated by comedy and romance. Barry McGuire's apocalyptic "Eve of Destruction" wasn't the first "death disc" to be banned on the grounds of bad taste (Ricky Valance's "Tell Laura I Love Her," the Shangri-Las' "Leader of the Pack," and Twinkle's "Terry" had all met similar opposition). It was not even a great record, being an unsubtle attempt to muscle in on the protest folk rock of Bob Dylan. But McGuire's anthem marked a crucial moment, raising the thorny issue of potential mass destruction within the confines of a mildly mesmerizing pop song.

As early as 1963, David Jones's growing sense of estrangement had manifested itself in one of his first serious attempts at songwriting, "Tired of My Life." His urge to wrap himself in the cloak of celebrity, entwined in his idolatry of his troubled older brother, was becoming morbid even before Terry's illness was recognized. And the sixteen-year-old was not merely world weary. A key line from the song (later resurrected as "It's No Game" on the 1980 *Scary Monsters* album) demonstrated the youngster's association of death with fame: "Put a bullet in my brain / And it makes all the papers."

Though he was briefly sucked into the "moon-and-June" language that was pop's mother tongue, the forbidden allure of destructive forces, both external and internal, has been a recurring theme in Bowie's work, even in his earliest years. While with the Konrads during 1962 and 1963, he had written songs based on news stories; inevitably, one was based on an air crash. And his November 1964 publicity stunt with the International League for the Preservation of Animal Filament had appealed to his sense of mischief, making him an agent of disruption on the easily riled surface of bourgeois culture.

While his misanthropic version of reality would find greater expression after he'd cut himself adrift from his early Beat pretensions, it was probably misanthropy as much as any obvious dramatic effect that prompted David Bowie and the Lower Third to incorporate Holst's "Mars—The Bringer of War" into their set during the mid-sixties. This menacing piece had been used as the theme for the second *Quatermass* series, a half-hour science-fiction drama first broadcast by BBC Television back in 1955. That series had introduced David Jones's generation to the perils—and for some, the splendid allure—of unknown forces from outer space hell-bent on the conquest and eventual destruction of Earth. Typical of fifties science fiction, *Quatermass* was an obvious metaphorical allusion to mankind's newfound capacity to self-destruct, and its huge popularity hinted at fears and panics never far away from the family home.

David Bowie's morbid fantasies were clearly stated in a *Melody Maker* profile in February 1966. It was billed chummily enough: "A Message to London from Dave," although by then, any post-Dylan "message" was suggestive of a kind of social critique. After a brief discussion of his desire to act, he provided a virtual line drawing of the ethos that would underpin much of his subsequent work, at least until the end of the seventies. "As far as I'm concerned," he began portentously, "the whole idea of Western life—that's the life we live now—is wrong. These are hard concepts to put into song, though."

That didn't prevent him from trying. In addition to contrasting the innocent joys of childhood with the disillusionment of adult life ("There Is a Happy Land"), his 1967 debut album was peopled with misfits. There was the bunged-up child murderer in "Please Mr. Gravedigger" (a Gothic tale complete with chiming church bells and thunderstorm sound effects). Another was the soldier in "Little Bombardier," who returns from war to unemployment and a descent into alcoholism. These vignettes of alienated men were overshadowed by "We Are Hungry Men," a plea to save the world from impending collapse caused by overpopulation and famine. "We are not your friends, we don't give a damn for what you're saying," sings Bowie, the potential savior, who is neatly juxtaposed with an authority figure barking out orders in classic Gestapo fashion. Even his observations on Swinging London, "Join the Gang" and "Maid of Bond Street," are unfashionably downbeat, with their cynical references to the "big illusion" and loneliness.

To characterize Bowie simply as a hopeless misanthrope, a Panglossian figure who pooh-poohs every magnaminious notion put forward by flower children in the year of universal love and peace, would be too reductive. A September 1967 profile that appeared in a local newspaper, *Chelsea News,* painted a quite different picture, that of an almost perfectly formed Love Child: "David is contented with contentment: he is a happy loving person with a gentle nature which reigns supreme over all agitation. He is the only person who I have met who brings nursery rhymes and fairy stories to the foreground of my mind." Bowie was beginning to learn to change masks at will.

In the summer of 1968, as student-inspired unrest in many of the world's large cities took all the headlines, Bowie, always one to hitch his observations to contemporary requirements, restated his earlier "Message to London." This time, in a three-part investigation by the *Times* into "The Restless Generation," he engaged in more finger pointing. Interviewed as part of the mixed-media Feathers trio, he told reporter Sheila More, "We feel our parents' generation has lost control, given up, they're scared of the future. . . . I feel it's basically their fault that things are so bad."

It was around this time that Bowie wrote *Ernie Johnson* in an attempt to introduce a comic (but conceptual) edge to the serious business of personal and social anxiety that was becoming apparent in his work. This, his first attempt at a sustained piece of writing, ended up in the trash. But the micro–rock opera, designed to flex his wider creative muscles, was an illuminating episode that merits more than a footnote in Bowie's career. Indeed, had he not been dropped by Decca in April, it is quite possible that *Ernie Johnson* might have been taken further than the demo stage.

The story of *Ernie Johnson* goes roughly as follows: Ernie wants to commit suicide, so he arranges a party for the big occasion. One of his guests is Tiny Tim, who'd recently gained notoriety for his bizarre performances on the *Rowan & Martin's Laugh-In* television show. The narrative then fractures into a series of cameos, each illustrated with a song. Ernie reminisces about Ann, "Nearly Jane," and Jill, his loves from the previous year. Ernie meets a tramp, with whom he discusses the "problem" of "nignogs." Ernie sings a song to himself in the mirror while smoking a joint (and ad-libs the intro thus: "Suicide isn't something I've always wanted to do . . . only the last couple of years. I mean, I'm not running away, I know who I am, I know what I'm made of"). Ernie arrives at a Carnaby Street boutique where he intends to purchase a tie. Whether he eventually hangs himself with it is not known, for the notes and songs run out before Ernie can deliver his tragicomic punchline. But it was a punchline that Bowie would return to again on *Ziggy Stardust*—with far-reaching consequences.

Ernie Johnson was quietly forgotten, and it was left for Major Tom, the astronaut Bowie launched into the pop cosmos with "Space Oddity," to become the first of Bowie's great fictional characters (though hardly a full-blown alter ego through which he would seek to resolve and expunge aspects of his personality). Though unashamedly inspired by Stanley Kubrick's film *2001: A Space Odyssey,* the song is ostensibly a tale about an astronaut who, through either mechanical failure or choice, is cast adrift in the solar system. His usual producer, Tony Visconti, might have thought it too musically lightweight, but lyrically, the song unites two of Bowie's recurring themes: the star trip and the death trip.

If Major Tom's successful liftoff had an air of wish fulfillment about it, phrases such as "you've really made the grade" and "the papers want to know whose shirts you wear" provided perfect metaphors for Bowie's own first big break. The song was metaphor rich indeed. Planet Earth may well be blue when viewed from outer space, but blue is also the color of melancholia, and when Bowie suffixes this line with "and there's nothing I can do," we're right in the achingly cold heart of Bowie's Weltanschauung. Read this way, the obvious conclusion is that the finale, where ground control has lost contact with Major Tom, who's now drifting away into space, is of Tom's own making.

More certain than ever before of the direction his own particular spaceship should take, Bowie was still unsure which musical stride to make next. The accompanying album, in many ways overshadowed by its lead track, eschewed the Bee Gees–flavored harmonies of the single in favor of a more eclectic feel, drawing on Dylan, the Beatles, acid rock, and even (on "Letter to Hermione") José Feliciano. Songs such as "An Occasional Dream" and "Memory of a Free Festival" betrayed Bowie's Beckenham artsy hippie trip, even if cerebral disturbance was rarely far away.

However, two songs from the album particularly stand out. "Cygnet Committee," an epic song with no obvious center, takes as many structural twists and turns as it offers viewpoints on Bowie's ever-changing world of ideas. The basic contradictions between these ideas are apparent near the song's end, where "I," "you," and "we" want to believe both "in the madness that calls now" and "that a light's shining through, somehow." Bowie, a beautiful young swan caught up in the conflicting torrents of cultural upheaval, battles his way through the "ruptured structures" of old, and the promises of false prophets using the language of revolutionary change—the "silent guns of love," the doors that must be unlocked, the "catholic throats" that must be slit, the dead child "laid slain on the ground." The anguish in his voice rudely undercuts any sense of neutrality in his moral dilemma.

This vision of imminent apocalypse even makes a reference to Terry and his predicament: "Screw up your brother, or he'll get you in the end." But it was another song, "Wild Eyed Boy from Freecloud," that really played out Terry's situation and that of any other mythical prophet figure he cared to imagine—or even himself. Discussing the song during a three-part Radio 1 documentary in 1993, Bowie quickly turned to his thoughts as a child: "Things and songs seemed to mean more to me than people . . . this feeling of isolation I've had ever since I was a kid was really starting to manifest itself through songs like that." Notwithstanding the schizophrenia that provides the track with its enduring motif ("really you and really me"), "Wild Eyed Boy from Freecloud" harks back to a preindustrial world where a boy lives alone outside a village on a mountainside. Mistrusted by the villagers, he is captured and imprisoned and sentenced to hang. But the mountain takes its revenge and engulfs the village, killing both the boy prophet and his captors.

For now, the notion of the beautiful, misunderstood outsider was given a fashionable hippie spin. But, as he entered a new decade—Bowie's "Art Decade," perhaps?—and with his own dreams of stardom given a surprise if welcome boost by the success of "Space Oddity," Bowie increasingly sought to create a space for himself (not Major Tom, whom he was happy to kill off) as a Major Rock 'n' roll Oddity. He already had the prototype fixed firmly in his head.

Of Ziggy
Stardust . . .

LIKE A LEPER MESSIAH, ZIGGY SUCKED UP INTO HIS MIND.

—"Ziggy Stardust," from *The Rise and Fall of Ziggy Stardust and the Spiders from Mars*

"The guy was unbelievable," Bowie told *Q* magazine's Paul Du Noyer in 1990. "He had this six-day party in some guy's house, that just went on and on. Just the weirdest kind of creature." That guy was Vince Taylor, a one-hit rock 'n' roller from that musical wasteland known as "Brit Beat Before the Beatles," roughly 1959–1962, an era that grows more fascinating with age. This was a time when David Jones immersed himself in popular music and Americana. Struggling with his own identity, he concluded, as did the main character in Jeanette Winterson's *Oranges Are Not the Only Fruit* (another tale of cultural estrangement and sexual identity), "I cannot recall a time when I did not know that I was special."

Vince Taylor was the ultimate Rise and Fall guy. And from the embers of Taylor's bizarre career, David Bowie found the seed that eventually blossomed into *The Rise and Fall of Ziggy Stardust.* "He always stayed in my mind as an example of what can happen in rock 'n' roll," Bowie told Du Noyer. "I'm not sure if I held him up as an idol or as something not to become. Bit of both, probably. There was something very tempting about him going completely off the edge. Especially at my age then, it seemed very appealing. Oh, I'd love to end up like that, totally nuts. Ha! Ha!"

It is tempting to suspect that Bowie was creatively immersed in rock 'n' roll mythology, and that his retelling of the Vince Taylor story was as much projection as it was founded on any real substance. But the facts of Taylor's life largely bear out his assessment.

Contrary to popular belief, Taylor was not an expatriate American at all, but Brian Maurice Holden, born in July 1939 to a working-class family in Isleworth, Middlesex. His family migrated to the United States after the war, first to New Jersey and then to California, where Brian first began singing onstage sometime around 1956. Adopting a new stage name, and sensing that Britain needed its own genuine rock 'n' roller, the self-styled Vince Taylor returned to London in 1957 and had no trouble surrounding himself with top musicians. (Tony Sheridan, who later recorded with the Beatles in Germany, and future Shadows Tony Meehan and Brian Bennett were early members of his backing band, the Playboys.)

Taylor's lasting legacy to rock 'n' roll is his April 1959 single, "Brand New Cadillac," the second of two glorious failures with Parlophone, who promptly dropped him. Although the cut (a B-side—it backed his cover of "Pledging My Love") was respected among genre aficionados, it was the Clash's rerecording on their album *London Calling* that popularized the song. Their version gave "Brand New Cadillac" added post-punk bite, but remained essentially faithful to Taylor's original.

Taylor, dark and handsome with slicked-back hair, soon found that continental Europe was far more receptive to his type of rock 'n' roll, already regarded as passé in Britain. Signing with a Belgian label, Palette Records, he scored a hit there with the presciently titled "I'll Be Your Hero." He wowed the Paris Olympia in July 1961 with a set based on tried-and-true Chuck Berry, Eddie Cochran, and Elvis Presley material, which shocked a country largely starved of genuine rock 'n' roll. The man in the spotlight, wielding a chain in his leather-gloved hand, handling the mike stand as if it was his only instrument of defense, crouched on one knee, mean, moody, and magnified, had found his audience. The French record label Barclay, sensing it had discovered its own Elvis Presley, signed him up for five years. The itinerant Taylor had found a home.

That winter, Vince was fêted in the manner of a true star, topping bills, appearing on television shows, and watching his records enter the French charts with satisfying regularity. Thrust into the limelight that had eluded him back in London, Taylor soon began to evince temperamental mood swings and took to occasionally preaching from the Bible onstage. Barry Hay, later vocalist with Dutch band Golden Earring, recalled seeing Taylor faint onstage during these years. Taylor also left a mark on future

New York Dolls frontman David Johansen, who recalled seeing him on American television during the mid-sixties: "The prototype rock 'n' roll star" was his verdict in 1974. Taylor had his own explanation: It was all an act. "Who am I?" he once asked rhetorically. "Jekyll and Mr. Hyde! As soon as I get on stage, I go out of myself, I lose control; often I lose consciousness. Afterwards, I become myself again."

Bowie first encountered Vince Taylor at the La Giaconda café in 1966. "The guy was right out of his tree," he told Radio 1's Kevin Howlett in 1993. "I mean, this guy was bonkers, absolutely the genuine article! I can't remember if he said he was an alien or the Son of God, but he might have been a bit of both. And he had all the sycophants believing him! He really did a number one job." There was one likely explanation for his behavior, as Rolling Stones associate Prince Stanislas Klossowski (alias "Stash") recalled in 1986. Returning to London in the mid-sixties, Taylor fell in with Dylan's touring entourage and future Velvet Underground icon Nico, survived on a diet of wine, acid, and speed, and generally "flipped out."

By the end of the decade, this kind of rock 'n' roll excess was commonplace. But in 1966, it was a revelation for Bowie, who had glimpsed an incipient madness in his half-brother and had perceived it in the mannerisms of Elvis, Little Richard, and Jerry Lee. Now, he was crouched on all fours outside of the Tottenham Court Road tube station in the heart of central London, staring at a map of the world, listening and watching as this deranged, ephemeral rock 'n' roller pointed out secret places where money was buried, where the aliens had their bases, and where he was going to build a new Atlantis. "I thought, 'There's something in this. I'm going to remember this. This is just too good!'" Bowie later recalled.

Taylor's dysfunctional rock-star trip didn't end there. By 1967, he was back in France trying to rebuild his career. Stash, who drummed for Taylor during this period, remembered exactly how this attempt at reconstruction manifested itself: "Vince started preaching to the public and voicing his mystic anxieties. Then we started playing as loud as we could in the hope that he would let go and begin singing. In the middle of 'Jezebel,' Vince started shouting like a banshee, throwing the mike on the ground, destroying everything around him." Another eyewitness account from Phil Guidal, author of a self-published Vince Taylor biography, *The Observatory,* described a performance for French TV program *Bouton*

Rouge as "a totally surrealistic experience by Vince," who "looks really diabolical, his body reacting to the music in a troubling mixture of animal sensuality and contained violence."

The uncontrollable urges that once gripped Vince Taylor under the bright lights now engulfed him completely. His 1967 tour was littered with incident. Often he'd leave the stage after three or four songs. Behind the scenes, those close to him sensed rapid deterioration, both in body and in mind. News of these performances travelled back to England, where they inevitably became magnified for dramatic effect. "At his last performance," Bowie told Du Noyer, "he dismissed the band, then went on stage dressed in white robes as Jesus Christ and said, 'I am the Resurrection, I am Jesus Christ.' They nearly lynched him there and then."

A perfect rock 'n' roll suicide, indeed, but Bowie's version—which also less self-consciously drew on Syd Barrett's sabotage of early Pink Floyd concerts and Peter Green's white-robed Manalishi/Messiah—wasn't quite true. After returning to England in the late sixties, and staying in a succession of rest homes, Taylor partially rebuilt his career, tailoring his act to biker crowds. In the month in which *Ziggy Stardust* appeared in Britain, June 1972, he released the album *Vince Is Alive, Well and Rocking in Paris,* though outside of cult French circles, nobody noticed. And that's the way it stayed for the rest of his life. Even death (in 1991), that surefire guarantee of rock 'n' roll infamy, couldn't massage Vince Taylor back to an iconic afterlife. Maybe Bowie himself doesn't realize that the man who provided one of the key building blocks for *Ziggy Stardust* is buried uncannily close to his own current center of activities, in Lutry, near Lausanne, in Switzerland.

TWO WISE MEN AND
A WOMAN

I NEVER THOUGHT I'D NEED SO
MANY PEOPLE.

—"Five Years," from *The Rise
and Fall of Ziggy Stardust and the Spiders from Mars*

NINETEEN SEVENTY WAS THE CUMU-
LATIVE YEAR FOR ME. THAT'S WHEN IT ALL
STARTED TO MAKE SENSE.

—on Radio 1, 1993

YOU KNOW I NEED SOME LOVING.

—"John, I'm Only Dancing," 1972

By the end of the sixties, the raw materials that would give the *Ziggy Stardust* album its defining shape were in place. Bowie had yearned for, and briefly experienced, stardom. A family of characters, many appropriated from the pop world, and one or two closer to home, existed inside his head, all manifestations of some abstract desire for personal estrangement. Many were unremarkable, catapulted by virtue of a minor talent into a butterfly net raised by the collective insanity of pop idolatry. More

important, in Bowie's eyes, were those who'd been twisted into awkward shapes by virtue of their inability—or unwillingness—to observe the rules of the game.

Although it is easy to see in Ziggy elements of all the casualties of the counterculture—especially Jimi Hendrix, Peter Green, and Syd Barrett—Bowie's later citing of the obscure Vince Taylor as his defining model was typical of his desire to wrap himself, and his work, in the cloak of mystery. At the start of 1970, he was being tipped for stardom of a more lasting kind than that afforded to a one-hit wonder: He was called rock's "Brightest Hope" in *Disc & Music Echo;* "Best Newcomer" in *Music Now;* and trumpeted with "A New Star Shoots Upwards" by pop pundit Penny Valentine. He had the looks and potential to become a big romantic singer in the manner of Scott Walker, wrote Anne Nightingale in the *Daily Sketch.* But any temptation to capitalize on the success of "Space Oddity" and

TWO WISE MEN AND A WOMAN   31 become the "Face of 1970" was tempered by his experiences on tour with the "Face of '68," Peter Frampton, who was not enjoying his time playing relentless boogie with Humble Pie. "I don't relish that idea of stardom very much," he told Nightingale. He then proved his point with a run of records that had little hope of maintaining a "pop" profile.

Relative to "Space Oddity," Bowie's work over the next eighteen months represented a baffling rejection of the success he had hankered after. Read against the longer view of his career trajectory, the subtext of which increasingly demanded infamy as a counterpoint to the simple joys of fame, his apparent retreat makes a lot more sense. In fact, his 1969 album was a far better barometer, a collection of disparate material bound by Bowie's wordiness (it was retitled *Man of Words, Man of Music* in America) relating themes of love and confusion. It was minstrelsy tailored toward a daydream nation.

The failure of that record bore out Tony Visconti's doubts about the wisdom of recording "Space Oddity." Since 1967, the long-playing record had developed into a creative entity in its own right, and the market had diverged accordingly. Pop artists worked within the tried-and-true confines of the three-minute single; those with more lofty "rock" aspirations looked increasingly toward the versatility of the full-length album as the appropriate vehicle for their complex musical ideas. Between March 1970 and January 1971, Bowie released three singles, "The Prettiest Star," "Memory of a Free Festival" (rerecorded version), and "Holy Holy," with little expectation that any of them would renew his fleeting affair with the pop market.

Ken Pitt, who had grown increasingly impatient with the man he'd been grooming for a successful public life, was baffled by what he saw as Bowie's profligate attitude. After having nursed him through the twilight years, encouraged his thirst for knowledge, and harangued a succession of record companies for underestimating the raw talent he was offering, he had become estranged from his charge. That "failed Afro" which Pitt did his best not to notice was only the first of many gestures that Bowie made to demarcate a growing independence. Falling in with Calvin Mark Lee, the hip young hustler who oversaw that traumatic Purcell Room concert, was another attempt to undermine Pitt's authority, which had grown increasingly precarious since the death of Bowie's father in August of 1969. (Pitt's stewardship of David's career had won the trust of John Jones, who had feared for his son's well-being in an unscrupulous industry.)

The catalyst in the eventual destruction of Pitt's relationship with Bowie was Angela Barnett, the first of three supporting characters without whom the entire Ziggy Stardust episode in David's career would have been still-born.

Angie, a Kingston Polytechnic economics and business studies student and a professional music industry hanger-on, began dating Bowie in April of 1969. At the time, he was nursing a badly damaged ego in the wake of Hermione's departure (in his own words, he was "bruised and insecure"), biding his time while Ken Pitt busily shopped the demo of "Space Oddity" around the major record companies. By most accounts, theirs was a see-what-you-can-do-for-me relationship from first sight: Bowie offered a handsome, aspiring pop figure, obviously talented but in need of a cheerleader or three; Angie represented someone more tuned in to understanding his increasingly outré aspirations.

The publication of two books that detailed her life with Bowie in rather lurid fashion, and an unforgettable talent for self-publicity that had her riding on his coattails during much of the seventies, has tended to diminish Angie's role in Bowie's life and work. But it is clear that infamy was as much on her agenda as it was on that of the man she married on 20 March 1970. She was a role-seeking hustler who would help organize Bowie's career in much the same way as June Bolan did for his friend and rival Marc Bolan (it is not insignificant that the Bolans had married two months earlier).

For Bowie, the go-it-alone Mod whose grandiose ventures always seemed to end with an even more self-conscious bump, the central lesson of the hippies' antiseptic karma was the need to feed off those around him. That didn't mean taking orders from a Ken Pitt father-figure type, who had provided both a mirror and stepladder for him to indulge his fantasies. During 1969 and 1970, he began to surround himself not with authority figures but with more youthful contemporaries, people who spoke his language and who could steer him into spaces he suspected were right for him. Angie, a brash and loud-talking young American woman with a feel for contemporary fashion and a propensity for modish sexual mores, was never a simple romantic partner to parade at parties and set up home with. She was the prop that gave him the confidence to confront the music industry for the first time. Together, they formed a unit where his sensitive, easily fractured exterior had the fast-talking foil necessary to confront the hard-nosed business he found himself in.

Angie was the grande dame of Haddon Hall, the magnificently named residence where the finer details of Bowie's cultural putsch were hatched. To the postman who delivered Bowie's infrequent checks and equally spartan fan mail, the address was more prosaic: Flat 7, 42 Southend Road, Beckenham. But the house's Edwardian fittings—molded ceilings, ornate tiled fireplace, stained-glass windows, minstrel's gallery and cellar—created a suitable ambience for the impoverished but aspiring newlyweds. When the checks started arriving, on the back of the success of "Space Oddity," the Bowies transformed their flat into something akin to the Old Curiosity Shop: red velvet curtains and matching upholstery, a huge Regency bed, antiquarian books, art deco vases, and other trophies of refinement.

When the pair moved into Haddon Hall in October 1969, "Space Oddity" was on its way up the charts, and Bowie's album for Philips was just weeks away from release. But the Humble Pie tour debacle and the album's relative failure forced Bowie to confront the wisdom of actively pursuing a solo career. A pickup backing band, Junior's Eyes, which had accompanied him on parts of the album and sometimes backed him in concert, represented little more than a casual relationship. neither did Bowie's next group, a four-piece band known as the Hype. But it did introduce him to the man who, for the next three years, would become the chief executor of Bowie's musical will.

The Axeman Cometh: Mick Ronson

Many insist that Mick Ronson was more than an executor; not least Bowie himself, who recently described the guitarist as "my Jeff Beck." For Beck was no simple sideman; he was a guitar hero, functioning at a time when guitar heroes were regarded with at least as much reverence as the frontmen. Ronson's recruitment to the team was, like Angie's, to bolster Bowie's standing. On a personal level, the two men were quite different, Ronson being unassuming and quietly creative, with a shyness that compelled the women in Bowie's circle to protect him. Musically, though, he was exactly the pillar of strength Bowie required, the first person he could call a genuine collaborator. After years spent looking beyond the simple confines of pop, Bowie had paired himself with someone steeped in the rough-and-tumble of guitar-led rock 'n' roll.

Born in Hull, Ronson shared few of the Beckenham Boy's inclinations toward self-absorption and artistic renown. A musical upbringing found him proficient on recorder, violin, and organ (which he played at a local Mormon church), and brought him, in his mid-teens, to the electric guitar. After spells with local beat and R&B bands the Mariners, the King Bees (a common beat moniker, it seems), and the Crestas, he set off to London to find fame and fortune. A liaison with the rock group the Voice, a front for the occult society the Process, was curtailed when he returned from a weekend visit to Hull to discover that the rest of the group had decamped to the West Indies. After a brief interlude playing soul covers with the Wanted, the despondent Ronson returned home.

One of the few Humberside bands fortunate enough to secure a record deal was the Rats, who once narrowly beat the Bowie-fronted Manish Boys in a "Best Local Groups" poll in the teenage girls' magazine *Mirabelle.* Despite a fluke appearance on the national television show *Thank Your Lucky Stars,* all roads led back to Hull, and by early 1966, the Rats were no more. Singer Benny Marshall and drummer Jim Simpson were reluctant to return to complete anonymity and decided to re-form the group before the year was out. Mick Ronson, then holding down a secure but dull job in a paint factory, jumped at the chance to join, and by April 1967, as the psychedelic summer approached, the Rats found themselves in Paris, playing a monthlong club residency. Hoping for similar exposure in London, the band spent a week there, huddled inside their van, before taking their deflated egos once again back to Hull.

After acquiring a new drummer, John Cambridge, in October 1967, and mindful of the trend toward studio-enhanced pop, the Rats cut an original track, "The Rise and Fall of Bernie Gripplestone." The track, which has only recently come to light, never got further than the master tape, but written records confirm that this was the original title, and that it was not concocted in a bid for some belated post–*Ziggy Stardust* glory. Apparently inspired by John Lennon's performance as Musketeer Bernard Gripweed in Dick Lester's film *How I Won the War,* the song— based on the chords of the Beatles' "Eleanor Rigby"—is full of period-piece charm, a dense, multitextured fog of backward drums (à la "Strawberry Fields Forever") and fuzzy guitar lines, in the style of the Jimi Hendrix Experience's "Love or Confusion."

Restrained in his interpersonal dealings, Mick Ronson was a demon unleashed when he had a guitar in his hand. And this studio debut was no exception, as subsequent Rats recordings reveal. Bowie's later declaration that Ronson was his Jeff Beck was no idle boast. For the fast-maturing guitarist had copped his entire repertoire from the ex-Yardbirds man, an influence that can be precisely dated to 17 March 1968. That's the day when the Rats traveled to Grantham to support the Jeff Beck Group, a London-based supergroup of sorts that provided a vehicle not only for Beck's increasingly flashy technique, but also for Rod Stewart's raucous vocal style. The Rats recorded the Beck Group's set on reel-to-reel tape and cheekily worked the songs into their own repertoire several months before Beck's album *Truth* hit the shops.

Two of these reworkings, of Tim Rose's "Morning Dew" and of "Jeff's Boogie" (suitably retitled "Mick's Boogie"), were recorded by the Rats early in 1969, together with a version of Gladys Knight and the Pips' "Stop and Get a Hold of Myself"; all survived on acetate and were later exhumed for a posthumous Rats collection. All three show Ronson to be a more than capable student of Beck's techniques: The double-tracked guitar effect, the short runs of spiralling notes, even the race-you-to-the-end climax of "Mick's Boogie" were straight out of Beck's bag of tricks. Little wonder, then, that Ronson was beginning to receive special billing in the band's publicity: "Featuring the fantastic guitar of Mike [*sic*] Ronson" proclaimed one gig poster.

The Rats, never a stable unit at the best of times, were further rocked when John Cambridge announced he was leaving to join London band Junior's Eyes. Cambridge was replaced by another local musician, Mick "Woody" Woodmansey, and the band pursued its heavy-rock direction with even more vigor, introducing into their set powerhouse versions of "Dazed and Confused" (popularized by Led Zeppelin), Hendrix's blues opus "Red House," and the Beatles' "Paperback Writer." Buoyed by his own improving technique, Mick Ronson even started performing in the manner of a guitar hero, picking his instrument with his teeth like a white Jimi Hendrix.

Fresh from another studio session, the Rats received a final blow when, late in January 1970, John Cambridge returned to Hull seeking his old guitar buddy. Mick Ronson was marking out lines on a rugby pitch when his London-based ex-colleague told him that David Bowie was looking for a guitarist for his new band. Ronson took the bait, and the pair first met at the Marquee, on 3 February, when 129 paying customers enjoyed some rare elbowroom at a show featuring Bowie as the headline act.

Two days later, Ronson was onstage with Bowie and Cambridge, with Tony Visconti on bass, recording a show for BBC Radio. According to the BBC's paperwork, Bowie's backing band was billed as the Tony Visconti Trio, but to all intents and purposes it marked the debut appearance of the Hype—the prototype Spiders. There was little time to rehearse (in the cellar at Haddon Hall, where Visconti and Cambridge were also now living), and Ronson's contribution was no more than perfunctory, in a set that began with Bowie strumming four songs solo. Ronson stuck capably to the recorded versions of "Janine" and "Wild Eyed Boy from Freecloud" from Bowie's recent album, and "The Prettiest Star," his just-recorded followup to "Space Oddity." But he came to life on "Unwashed and Somewhat Slightly Dazed" and a new song, "The Width of a Circle," tossing in typical guitar-hero breaks of Beck-like intensity. For these brief moments, it was almost shocking to hear Bowie removed from the action; for the first time in his post–beat group career, he had submerged himself in a powerhouse rock-band sound. Audiences now had two reasons to enjoy David Bowie: for his troubador artistry and for the instrumental dexterity of his backing band.

Fearing that any false move might jeopardize the precarious course of his gently inclining career, Bowie didn't wholeheartedly embrace his backup group. In fact, eighteen months passed before he decided to throw his hat in with a fully functioning band. Until then, he had kept his options open, recording with the band but crediting the records to himself; playing live with a group under the Hype banner, but sometimes performing solo; writing songs and then offering them to other artists with the potential to turn them into hits; and even occasionally venturing into the role of artistic director, "creating" stars from the chosen within his social circle. In time, this esoteric approach would enhance his auteur status,

but for now it merely proved a source of continual frustration to those around him.

The battle was one of idealism versus realism. In his mind, Bowie still subscribed to a go-it-alone approach, where he would be untroubled by compromises like the ones he had been forced to make during his early career. But the job market for solo singers was already narrowing to the distinctly un-showbiz genre of singer-songwriter. This market was led by such Canadians and Americans as Joni Mitchell, James Taylor, and Leonard Cohen, whose predilections for self-analysis were far too naked and "honest" to satisfy Bowie's long-term creative impulses. None of them would have concerned themselves with a project as dubious as the Hype, let alone name a band after such a maligned concept.

In an interview with Raymond Telford for *Melody Maker,* published in the 28 March 1970 edition, Bowie explained the rationale behind the group's name and the Hype's relationship to his own career. "I deliberately chose the name in favor of something that sounded perhaps heavy, because now no one can say they're being conned. . . . I suppose you could say I chose it deliberately with tongue-in-cheek." That same month, a group of nearly a hundred British journalists were flown to the United States to witness the debut of a new band called Brinsley Schwartz, whom they promptly attacked as being overly puffed by "dishonest" record-company marketers. Clearly Bowie's embrace of hype revealed his counter-revolutionary tendencies.

The Hype experience held Bowie in good stead, not only for its unashamed and knowing embrace with unhip but inescapable marketing strategies. The band also flouted another golden rule of the rapidly expanding, though downwardly (and dourly) attired progressive market, by daring to walk onto a stage dressed gaily in an assortment of comic-book

GEM Presents

DAVID BOWIE LIVE!

+ BOB (Sounds of the 70s) HARRIS

at EBBISHAM HALL, EPSOM
SATURDAY, MAY 27th

Tickets 50p   Doors open 7.30 p.m.

costumes. The band's public debut was as support to Fat Mattress, a dull hard-rock vehicle formed by Jimi Hendrix bassist Noel Redding in an unsuccessful attempt to step out of the great man's shadow.

With Ken Pitt increasingly uninterested in playing a peripheral part catering to Bowie's promotional needs, there was little fanfare for the concert, which took place on 22 February at London's underground mecca, the Roundhouse. Expectations were virtually nil. And so was the reaction, despite the appearance of four grown men dressed in costume, as Hypeman (Tony Visconti in a modified Superman outfit), Cowboyman (John Cambridge), Gangsterman (Mick Ronson in a fedora and a gold lamé suit), and Rainbowman (a scarf-bedecked Bowie).

Bowie has since insisted that "theater was for me after that [concert]," but the reality of his post-Hype existence fails to bear this out. In fact, rock theater was the last thing on his mind during the next few months, as he struggled to establish himself on a sound business footing, vacillating between furthering his own solo career and becoming first among equals in a rock group that embraced values that ran counter to those of the prevailing musical culture. For the time being, he chose not to embrace the enemy—the four-piece rock-band format he had been resisting since early 1967. Instead, he ran straight into the arms of the third and final member of his management-production team: Tony Defries, The Man Who Would Sell the World David Bowie.

The Salesman: Tony Defries

There is no better evidence that Bowie was intensely insecure about his musical direction in the aftermath of "Space Oddity" than the testimony of Tony Visconti, producer, arranger, bassist (and probably a lot more) during sessions for *The Man Who Sold the World,* which was recorded during April and May of 1970. In 1994, recalling the making of the album, he insisted that Bowie was "so frustrating to work with at this time: I couldn't handle his poor attitude and complete disregard for his music." The producer attributed this to three things: "Discovering love deeply with Angela, his dissatisfaction with Ken Pitt, and mainly the new money he had in his pockets from his first ever hit." Any early enthusiasm for an album that would be, in Visconti's words, "our *Sgt. Pepper,*" soon degenerated into confusion, with Bowie, the record's center, often absent. "I had to peel them [the newlyweds] apart to get David to listen to what the band had just done, or to get him to do a vocal—or even finish the lyrics," remembered an exasperated Visconti.

Although a hindrance musically, Angie Bowie was instrumental in organizing Bowie behind the scenes, obtaining much of the cash that would finance the making of the album by securing a deal for the Hype that was independent of Bowie's solo contract with Philips/Mercury. While hustling for money, which required a meeting with Olav Wyper, general manager at Philips, Angie had encouraged David to see Wyper and explain the Ken Pitt "problem." There was no question that the manager, whose belief in Bowie had left him considerably short of money, had the best intentions for his protégé. It was simply that his enthusiasm was woefully misplaced in the new rock order into which Bowie was headed. Wyper supplied the names of three lawyers who might be able to resolve the obstacle, including that of his own legal adviser, Tony Defries.

Bowie first discussed his predicament with Defries in March 1970. At the same time, in another part of central London, the Beatles were gearing up to engage in a similar legal battle as they sought to extricate themselves from the heavy burden of Apple Corps, and from each other. Bowie explained to the eager and relatively young businessman how he'd outgrown Pitt's way of working, and how Pitt had been pointing him in the wrong direction, so much so that the Bowies had turned to an independent concert promoter, NEMS, simply to find suitable places to play.

Defries, who was a managing clerk of litigation at the Godfrey Davis and Batt law firm, and whose only management experience had been handling the careers of several London fashion models, advised Bowie to write to Pitt, stating that he was no longer his personal manager. He then introduced Bowie to Laurence Myers, a showbiz accountant with aspirations of breaking into more creative endeavors, such as artist management. Gem Productions, based on Regent Street in central London, took a leap of faith, adding Bowie, the New Seekers, and Gary Glitter to its books during 1970. All three investments would reap considerable rewards in the months ahead.

Surprisingly, at least to Myers and Defries, who were utterly convinced of his artistic attributes, Bowie's gestation period would be the longest. Arguably, the man who underwent the most significant changes during the rest of the year was Tony Defries. The neat and conservatively dressed legal man who stepped into Ken Pitt's office on 5 May to tie up loose ends had, by November, effected a Bowie-like transformation. When Pitt visited him on 8 December, he noticed that his successor (Defries had by this time assumed the role of Bowie's manager, under the auspices of Gem) had transformed into what Pitt described as "the last of the sixties' swingers, complete with roll-top sweater, neck chains, hanging medallions and Afro hairstyle." The man, like his apprentice, fully understood the importance of playing the part.

The financial aspects of Bowie's trust in Defries would not affect him for some years. The essential point is that a seemingly sound, if ultimately corrosive, business plan had been put into action by the manager, and that Bowie, who tended to magnify cherished associates beyond their real worth, had complete confidence in his abilities. He could now get down to the creative aspects of career-building. Visconti has emphasized the importance of the "security and advice" aspect of Defries's role: "Angie and Defries are often maligned by critics and cronies of David, but without their constant support and input, there would never have been a Ziggy, or an Aladdin, or a future Bowie for that matter."

NEW DECADE/ART DECADE

I'M SO WIPED OUT WITH THINGS AS
THEY ARE.

**—"Star," from _The Rise and
Fall of Ziggy Stardust and the Spiders from Mars_**

PROGRESSIVE [MUSIC] HAS FEELING, AND IS
CREATED FOR THE SATISFACTION OF THE WRITER OR
MUSICIAN FIRST. POP MUSIC IS HUMOROUS AND TIT-
ILLATES THE MIND AND IS CREATED FOR THE STUPID,
UNTHINKING RECORD-BUYING PUBLIC.

**—Letter from S. Peake from
Worthing, Sussex, to _Melody Maker,_ 19 August 1972**

Stardust in Stasis

During 1970 and 1971, David Bowie had it all: Angie, Defries, and an incipient musical partnership with Mick Ronson. But for much of this watershed period he was invisible. To those around him, he was waiting in the wings; to the rest of the world, as memories of "Space Oddity" faded, he had been consumed by pop's black hole, one more one-hit wonder to be pulled out at pub quizzes at some future point. Like the stylophone that he used on that single, and that was eagerly promoted in magazine advertisements to ride on the single's success, Bowie was per-

42

ceived as a fleeting novelty act, cast aside by the prevailing trends of the new decade.

The drives that fueled pop at the start of the seventies were institutional and cultural. First, the rapidly growing chasm between the singles (pop) and albums (rock) markets was a logical conclusion of the fallout from 1967. The notion of pop as art, which had been given a significant boost by the technical and mock-conceptual achievements of the Beatles' *Sgt. Pepper* album in 1967, had given pop musicians—tripping on imagination-enhancing drugs such as LSD—the idea that songs needn't be restricted by time or theme. Cloaked in a protective purplish haze, they hid themselves away inside increasingly high-tech studios, fitted out with eight-track, and soon sixteen-track, recording consoles.

Where studios once resembled doctors' offices, where men in white coats took the patient's pulse and marked it down for posterity before

swiftly ushering in the next, they now became long-stay sanitoriums, where the psyche was put through its paces. Increasingly, the patients took the equipment home with them in search of their own prognosis. Or perhaps prog/gnosis, for the emphasis was on progression—bigger, better, louder—and self-knowledge; a desperate search for that proverbial lost chord.

Pop's increasing need for pills to purge itself of its commercially induced ills was caused by an irreconcilable contradiction, increasingly apparent as the late sixties rock counterculture was forced to let go of its impossible dream. The cultural freedoms set in motion by the hippie subculture had enjoyed a clear relationship with developments in sound alteration and the structural collapse of the traditional verse/chorus discipline of the three-minute pop song. But like the butterfly that symbolized it, the new dawn barely got past sunrise, wilting on the barricades in Paris and Chicago before being trampled underfoot in the rush to cling to something more tangible.

It was Tim Hardin who had posed the question "how can we hang on to a dream?" Among artists, there was a large enough pile of burned-out bodies to suggest that psychedelia had exacted a high price on many of its most enthusiastic trail blazers. Pockets of idealism hung on in sections of San Francisco and London, where bands such as Quintessence and Hawkwind lived together and played for free whenever they could. But the general trend, particularly in America, was toward gigantism:

huge fee-paying festivals, where the main attractions were either hard-rocking, blues-based virtuosos (Mountain, Grand Funk Railroad, Led Zeppelin) displaying absolute mastery over their instruments, or else singer-songwriters (Joni Mitchell, Melanie, Leonard Cohen) retreating into the "truth" of their relationships and laying bare their vulnerabilities for earnest audiences.

Two extremes: Hard rock flattered the audience with an overbearing sense of its own power, while the six-string bards lent a sense of psychological maturity. Both were transatlantic phenomena. But pop heartlands also developed their own traits. In the United Kingdom, the notion of technical expertise was nailed by some groups to the European classical tradition, with bands such as Yes, King Crimson, the Moody Blues, and ELP harnessing the electronic revolution to their aspirations as legitimate composers. MC5 manager and White Panthers spokesman John Sinclair might have declared that "rock is a weapon in the cultural revolution," but he presumably had more in mind than simply joining the high art tradition of bourgeois culture. The story was different in the States, where many of the leading lights of acid rock (the Grateful Dead, Quicksilver, the Byrds) followed Dylan and the Band into country rock.

At the heart of this proliferation of styles was a desire to elude the vagaries of the commercial pop market, a market that continued to throw up cheery, sing-along bubblegum outfits that provided immediate comfort rather than confronting listeners with beard-tugging problems. The contradiction, though, was that real money was being generated where the new, earnest musos worked—in huge-grossing concert tours and highly prof-

itable albums. The seven-inch single wasn't yet the loss-leader it is today, but sales of albums had eclipsed those of the 45 by the start of the seventies, buoyed by an older, more affluent middle-class audience. Columbia Records coined the phrase "the Man can't bust our music" in a shamefaced bid to win over the wavering underground, but "the Man can't help but sell shitloads of our music" would have been more appropriate. The counterculture was sold on the idea of conspicious consumption.

The thrusting power chords of cock-rock, the rustic ambience of hoedown harmonies, the twelve-string bedroom minidramas, and the symphonic whine of the monstrously sized banks of keyboards were all benchmarks of a growing alienation from the teen constituency symbolic of rock's aspirant, upwardly mobile status. This is exactly what David Bowie was referring to when he appeared on the *Dinah Shore Show* in May 1977 and declared, "I think I wiped out the sixties"; he had helped bring this dull partisanship to its knees with the *Ziggy Stardust* album.

The loss of the Beatles, who before their acrimonious split early in 1970 had been the one band able to straddle the growing pop/rock divide, robbed popular music of its unity, however fragile it had been. For all the talk of shunning the plastic puppetry of their pop pasts and embracing the real concerns of love, social awareness, and spirituality, the biggest fantasy of all was epitomized by the angriest ex-Beatle, John Lennon, tucked away in his Surrey mansion imagining he had no possessions. Fab John's dream was over, and so were the dreams of the generation for which he had tired of being a spokesman.

Even the sexual freedoms that had accompanied the opening of the gates of Eden had developed not along fashionable unisex lines, but on hideous caricatures of mainstream stereotypes. Bare-chested, masculine icons, such as Robert Plant, Paul Rodgers, and Roger Daltrey, stalked the world's stages as hybrids of Lord Byron and Tarzan, while gaggles of groupies waited backstage, ready and willing to massage their triumphant wills. Rock appeared to be a man's world; pop was its feminine opposite, there to be chewed up and spat out. So much for the Age of Aquarius.

The Unbearable Seriousness of Moonlight

Just as rock's beautiful balloon was being badly punctured by death and fragmentation, David Bowie—an absorber as well as an observer of contemporary drifts—was also afflicted by uncertainty. Niche marketing was becoming the order of the day, which was fine if you understood which category you fit: bubblegum pop, country rock, progressive rock, hard rock, or singer-songwriter. But where now for a one-hit wonder with nihilist tendencies, whose aspirations of greatness encompassed songwriting genius, musical invention, and, more than either, a dramatic and highly developed sense of his own apartness?

The road to Ziggy, which had been glimpsed with the theatrical-rock experiment that was the Hype, was seemingly blocked after Bowie retreated back to Haddon Hall for the rest of 1970 and the early months of 1971. It was as if he'd washed his hands of his own proactivity, handing the reins of his career to those around him. Tony Visconti had gone, dismayed by David's lackadaisical attitude during sessions for *The Man Who Sold the World* and by his eager recruitment of Tony Defries to mastermind his career for him. And Mick Ronson had returned to Hull, taking Woody Woodmansey (who'd replaced John Cambridge for the album sessions) with him.

With his own rise temporarily on hold, the sense of fall had also revisited Bowie on a more personal level. After several years' absence, Terry, the half-brother who'd been cast adrift by the family and now had nowhere else to go, began staying at Haddon Hall for weeks at a time. This confrontation with the man almost ten years David's senior, whose distance had turned him into a fantasy object for the young David, was a salutary reminder of Terry's vulnerability.

By this time, Terry had become a patient at the Cane Hill Hospital, a grim Victorian institution, where he was treated for schizophrenia with the usual array of mind-numbing remedies. Bowie, who'd long equated creative urges with a kind of mental illness, found the entire experience uncomfortable, his attitude toward Terry's predicament remaining hopelessly inconsistent. Sometimes he was protective, rescuing Terry from wandering into potentially dangerous situations on more than one occasion, but he could also find Terry's predicament too much to handle. Matters reached a head one night early in 1971 when, finding a disheveled and obviously disturbed Terry on her doorstep, his aunt Pat drove Terry to Beckenham to obtain the required doctor's recommendation for readmission to Cane Hill. Finding the hospital closed, she took Terry to David's for the night, only to be told that David was "busy." The next time the brothers met, in the summer of 1982, Terry was in the hospital recovering from a suicide attempt. On 16 January 1985, Terry Burns walked out of Cane Hill and threw himself under a moving train.

The card that David sent along with flowers for the funeral read, "You've seen more things than we could imagine" (adapted from Rutger Hauer's last lines in *Blade Runner*). It was a double-edged reminder that, despite the obvious pain and misery of his estranged half-brother's mental state, there was an element of Terry's condition that Bowie believed afforded him a privileged status in the world. This was emphatically stated on "All the Madmen," one of the key songs on *The Man Who Sold the World* (and indeed in Bowie's entire canon), an album that, rather appropriately, was issued in three strikingly different sleeves during the early months of 1971.

With its references to "friends" locked "in mansions cold and gray" on "the far side of town," "All the Madmen" is unmistakably based on Terry's incarceration at Cane Hill. Setting up an opposition between "the madmen" and "the sadmen roaming free," between "the thin men" who "stalk the streets / While the sane stay underground," Bowie wholeheartedly equates himself with the asylum-seekers, a further manifestation of his continuing desire to escape from—and to critique—the flat and sad personalities on the outside, safe in the knowledge that the nonconformists are locked away out of sight and, inevitably, out of their minds.

The gentle escape effected on "Space Oddity" was given an increasingly morbid and violent twist on much of *The Man Who Sold the World*. Witness the Vietnam veteran in "Running Gun Blues" (based on a true story), who, having been trained by the state, just can't stop killing; the "strange, mad celebration" of an immortal, unhampered by petty morality, in "The Supermen"; misplaced trust in false gods promising utopia but delivering boredom in "Saviour Machine"; the crushed romance of "She Shook Me Cold"; and the sea of nonbelief in "After All." The album was

48   THE RISE AND FALL OF ZIGGY STARDUST AND
      THE SPIDERS FROM MARS

also notable for the introduction of the Bowie doppelganger, a monster that, on close inspection, "was me," in the opening "The Width of a Circle." What could have been *The Man Who Saved the World* was, in Bowie's hands, something much uglier, the implication being that the morally bankrupt world, like everything in the universe, was available if the price was right.

VELVET GOLDMINE,
OR SEX AND THREADS AND
ROCK 'N' ROLL

I COULD MAKE A TRANSFORMATION
AS A ROCK 'N' ROLL STAR.

—"Star," from *Ziggy Stardust
and the Spiders from Mars*

SO OFTEN IT'S NOT MY POINT OF VIEW I'M
PUTTING ACROSS. I'M MORE LIKE A FOCAL POINT FOR
A LOT OF IDEAS THAT ARE GOIN' AROUND.
SOMETIMES I DON'T FEEL LIKE A PERSON AT ALL. I'M
JUST A COLLECTION OF OTHER PEOPLE'S IDEAS.

—to Mick Rock, *Rolling Stone*,
June 1972

DRESS MY FRIENDS UP JUST FOR SHOW
SEE THEM AS THEY REALLY ARE.

—"Andy Warhol," from *Hunky Dory*

David Bowie, June 1972,
Oxford Town Hall, England
MICK ROCK, COURTESY OF
STAR FILE

51

At the end of 1970, just weeks before *The Man Who Sold the World* was released in America (it appeared in the United Kingdom months later, in April 1971), David Bowie was asked by the *New Musical Express* to name his favorite singer. His choice was Iggy Pop, frontman of the Stooges, a band another paper had once dismissed as "pimply rubbish rock." While Bowie had long struggled for an onstage persona to match his distinctly jaundiced worldview, Iggy, a festering sore on the old ideals of the counterculture, was a real-life, leather-trousered misanthrope.

Taking Jim Morrison's riot-inciting antics several stages further, to a point where self-immolation became art, Iggy had achieved notoriety earlier that year when he had acted in defiance of gravity, walking across the hands of the crowd at the Cincinnatti Pop Festival (an event that was televised across America). Only this wasn't a man intent on healing the world. Iggy Pop was a veritable Antichrist, elevating trash culture and self-abuse into an art form. While his band ground out simplistic guitar riffs at maximum volume, Iggy would taunt his audience with broken bottles before turning the serrated glass on himself, carving wounds on his body as if to reflect his mental state. Just in case the message was lost on anyone, this living, bleeding showman would throw up onstage before exiting to indulge himself in further feats of self-abuse.

Bowie's discovery of Iggy Pop wasn't his first encounter with those who looked out on the American Dream and saw only a nightmare. In November 1966, Ken Pitt had flown to New York and been introduced to pop art wunderkinde Andy Warhol, with a view to becoming the London promoter for both Warhol and the Velvet Underground, the house band at Warhol's studio, the Factory. That particular venture foundered in spite of Pitt's best efforts, but on his return home, he passed David his acetate copy of the band's first album, which had been given to him by their songwriter, Lou Reed.

Bowie occasionally name-dropped the Fugs album that Pitt had also brought home with him, even going as far to incorporate their "Dirty Old Man" into his act. But he seemed to keep the Velvets under his hat, despite recording a version of the band's "Waiting for the Man" with the Buzz as early as December 1966. His cover was brusque and considerably more decorative than the mantralike original. He also saw fit to insert an additional bit of London camp into the song: "I'm just looking for a good friendly behind." Another track from that criminally overlooked first

Velvets album, "Venus in Furs," received the Bowie treatment when he lifted the chorus (and some of the lyrics) wholesale for his own "Little Toy Soldier." Both recordings were discarded but have since entered into circulation on bootlegs (found most easily on the *Pierrot in Turquoise* bootleg CD).

The Velvet Underground, hyped-up, would-be stars of Warhol's mixed-media show the Exploding Plastic Inevitable, pioneered caterwauling minimalism, an adjunct of developments in the rarefied world of classically trained modernism. Hiding behind dark shades and theatrical devices such as whip-wielding dancers, they bombed on the West Coast, where they were treated like the unwelcome invaders from the brutal streets of New York that they were, the antithesis of California sunshine music. But that wasn't the Velvets' only strength. Lou Reed's songwriting was, like Bowie's, observational and character filled, though rooted in a gritty realism that often eluded the Englishman.

If the aesthetic of these American miscreants was far more suited to Bowie's Weltanschauung than to those of his British contemporaries, it is obvious why he took so long to make the connection manifest: The fit of the Stooges' and the Velvets' brutally reductive sound with Bowie's singer-songwriterly demeanor and Eurocentric musical perspective was as ungainly as it was unlikely. But it is notable that as soon as Bowie plugged in with his hard-hitting four-piece Hype for a BBC Radio session in April 1970, he chose to perform "Waiting for the Man," albeit with an upbeat, vaguely progressive demeanor.

While these musical references would loom large in the formation of the *Ziggy Stardust* sound during the months ahead, the strongest pull came from the idea of incorporating a theatrical element into the presentation of his delicate self. This had been an enduring passion of Bowie's ever since the mid-sixties, when he had fantasized about future film stardom, settling instead for hiding behind the pancake in Lindsay Kemp mime productions.

The sleeve of *The Man Who Sold the World* was to be his grand entrance into the seventies. Jettisoning the design he'd originally commissioned, which depicted a rifle-toting John Wayne type standing outside Cane Hill, he hit upon the idea of a dramatic iconic portrait of himself, reclining on a couch wearing a dress—a man's dress, as he was later to correct inquisitive journalists. As it happened, America went with the original sleeve (airbrushing out a few words in a speech bubble that could be construed to condone drug-taking). In Britain, where the sleeve won him some national press in the *Daily Mirror,* the record sank with barely a snigger. *Gay News* began to track his movements, but features in *Melody Maker* ("Why Does David Bowie Like Dressing Up in Ladies' Clothes?"), *New Musical Express* ("I'm Not Ashamed of Wearing Dresses"), and *Disc* (which couldn't resist titling its piece "Why Bowie Is Feeling Butch") failed to translate into sales.

Despite preferring to pass on the "dress" sleeve, it was America that first picked up on the new aesthetic forming in Bowie's head, the one he'd worn so spectacularly on his body during his promotional visit there in February 1971. "Space Oddity" had not been a hit there, so his arrival was not tainted with the cynicism British rock journalists reserved for someone they merely regarded as an attention-seeking pop pretender.

Perhaps it was the thrill of finally making it across to the land of milk, honey, Elvis, and Warhol that sharpened his thought processes. Or a fulmination reached after months spent absorbing influences and rethinking strategies. Whatever the case, Bowie began to articulate the raw matter of an incipient counter-ideology that within two years would make him the most visible rock star of the seventies. Speaking to *Rolling Stone* writer John Mendelsohn, he started to encapsulate fifteen years' worth of fan worship and self-love into a coherent philosophy that would underpin his own launch into heroism.

Mendelsohn's feature, titled "David Bowie: Pantomime Rock," begins with obvious references to Bowie's chosen mode of attire, the "velvet midi-gown," and how "he would prefer to be regarded as a latter-day Greta Garbo." After the London *ubermensch* expresses his revulsion of the "mediocre," he carves out a niche for himself, in turn redefining the practice of the rock artist: "There's enough fog around," he says. "That's why the idea of performance-as-spectacle is so important to me." His conclusion is even more devastating. "What the music says may be serious, but as a medium it should not be questioned, analysed or taken so seriously. I think it should be tarted up, made into a prostitute, a parody of itself. It should be the clown, the Pierrot medium. The music is the mask the message wears—music is the Pierrot and I, the performer, am the message."

On his return to London, Bowie continued this theme, albeit in more streamlined fashion, to George Tremlett: "I'm going to become much more theatrical, more outrageous. Much more outrageous than Iggy and the Stooges have ever been." As yet, only the dress provided any real evidence of this. Two months later, though, his remarks to Mendelsohn began to reveal their true Warholian colors.

Coming on as a full-blown superstar in America, Bowie returned to the bitter reality of second-rate status in Britain. That was confirmed in the summer, when he was booked alongside the band of ex–Incredible String Band man Mike Heron for a BBC Radio "In Concert" broadcast. It was the public debut of the band-who-would-become-the-Spiders, though you wouldn't have known it from the performance, which was akin to a rock 'n' roll revue, with David ostensibly the man holding it all together. The recently recalled Mick Ronson and Woody Woodmansey, together with fellow Humberside man Trevor Bolder, were announced as members of Ronno, who, according to emcee John Peel, were about to start recording an album. An assortment of vocalists took center stage at various times during the show: Two new songs, "Song for Bob Dylan" and "Andy Warhol," were sung by George Underwood and Dana Gillespie, respectively, while Geoffrey Alexander led a version of a Chuck Berry crowd-pleaser, "Almost Grown." Bowie wasn't exactly relegating himself to the sidelines; he was still left with "The Supermen" and four new songs, "Queen Bitch," "Bombers," "Looking for a Friend," and "Kooks," along with a little-known cover, "It Ain't Easy." To confuse matters, John Peel was also asked to introduce Mark Carr Pritchard (who sang "Looking for a Friend") as a member of a band called Arnold Corns, who'd just recorded a single called "Moonage Daydream."

The broadcast was a grand gesture, no doubt deliberately so, as Bowie tried out his newfound "Pierrot medium," bringing the notion of play to his own artistry. The material was as disparate as he could have made it, though the influence of New York was increasingly apparent. "Looking for a Friend" wasn't too far removed from the Velvet Underground's "Waiting for the Man." "Queen Bitch," which opened the set, had the makings of the finest Lou Reed song he never got to write. And "Andy Warhol," with its life-as-pantomime line "Dress my friends up just for show / See them as they really are," confirmed the exact location of the neophyte's new artistic watering hole.

At the opening of his own art show in London in 1995, Bowie paid tribute to Warhol, describing him as "one of the most influential and important artists of the second half of this century." In seeking to explain why, he offered a sweeping cultural brushstroke: "His ability was to confuse art enough that the boundaries started coming down, so there was no division between high and low art." Back in 1971, he might have seen Warhol's example in more narcissistic terms. Like Bowie's, Warhol's favored themes were celebrity and disaster. On occasion, usually at crucial moments in their careers—Warhol's multiple-image depiction of Jackie Kennedy after her husband's assassination, Bowie's *Ziggy Stardust* venture—these coincided. And like Bowie's, Warhol's relationship with disaster was bound up with a strong sense of his own mortality. Both feared flying and the prospect of a violent death (in Bowie's case, he exorcised the former after the Ziggy period, but, after John Lennon's murder in 1980, tellingly went underground for the best part of three years). Warhol, too, fell in love with the idea of celebrity at an early age, "collecting" idols such as movie star Elizabeth Taylor and socialite Truman Capote.

Most of all, Warhol, like Bowie, was interested in people, or at least people-as-manifesting-ideas. And just as Warhol did indeed blur the boundaries of high and low art, he also blurred the ideas of the artist and his work, so much so that it is impossible to disengage the two when discussing one or the other. As the spate of newspaper tributes celebrating Bowie's fiftieth birthday have shown, he too has wrapped his personality around his work to such a degree that any clear separation has become almost impossible.

In a way, there was nothing new about such an idea in pop music, which had always been as much about selling personalities as music. What Bowie did was introduce an element of self-reflection to this idea, making overt the construction of "the star," while at the same time throwing the hitherto uncomplicated idea of identity into crisis. Rock romanticism, which clung to the notion of art as a series of existential decisions reached for from within, would never again be quite the same. That Bowie fully understood it this way in mid-1971 is unlikely. He certainly did later on, telling Charles Shaar Murray, "It's much more of a realism for me to think that this [he gestured towards his hair, his clothes, the room] is all me, that there's nothing else in here. It's all outside."

The significance of Warhol's aesthetic sensibilities certainly affected Bowie, and rock culture at large, at a deeper level as *Ziggy Stardust* was played out during 1972 and 1973. For the time being, though, Bowie appropriated—rightly, given the nature of Warhol's credo—the surface workings of this artist-as-absent-center. Speaking on Radio 1 in 1993, he suggested that he was duped by the idea of Warhol as a nonperson: "I bought this whole pop art thing that he wasn't a real person, that he was just this creation." But given Bowie's predilection for identifying with magnified personalities, most of whom were repositories for his own self-transcending fantasies, the enigma of this living vacuum doubling as a creative center provided a near-perfect role model.

Andy Warhol signified everything that Bowie could ask for in his contradictory fix on stardom. The artist was at once star and antistar, an icon renowned for not speaking (or, better still, getting others to speak on his behalf), which only served to enhance his aura of detachment. Famous for depersonalized art that drew on already existing source material such as Coke bottles and Campbell's soup cans, Warhol was even more cherished for his depersonalized self, an objet d'art that neatly reflected the world of surfaces in which he (or, more likely, his never-ending stream of assistants) worked.

This bleached-out, notoriously bewigged, and apparently sexually indifferent human artwork, who chose to observe the world through an ever-present pair of sunglasses, extended his art-as-artifice design by surrounding himself with the living tinsel of those he designated, in fairy-godmother fashion, "superstars." Wrapped up in the "everybody will be famous for fifteen minutes" aphorism, most of these were larger-than-life street characters, whose presence at the Factory provided Warhol with a twenty-four-hour soap opera played out by a cast of transvestites, drug addicts, and assorted loudmouths.

Bowie got his first taste of the Andy Warhol freak show in August 1971, when a stage production detailing life at the Factory hit London for a six-week run. Titled *Pork,* it was based on numerous telephone conversations that had been recorded by the artist and transcribed, edited, and rearranged by director Tony Ingrassia. Minor "superstars," including Wayne County (Vulva/Viva), Tony Zanetta (Warhol), and Cherry Vanilla (Pork/Brigid Polk), played the roles of the "real" superstars as a slice of Warhol's New York came to London in fictionalized form.

The show, part of the self-styled "ridiculous theater" genre that enjoyed a temporary vogue in New York, soon attracted the attention of the tabloid press. Alerting the public to its sensational content—Masturbation! Abortion! Drugs! Fetishistic Sex! Transvestites!—only served to boost audiences, who arrived at the Roundhouse to be greeted by warning signs: "If you are likely to be disturbed, please do not attend." Most who did were confused rather than titillated by the interminably daft series of vignettes, as the cast of New York crazies darted around a wheel-chair-bound "Warhol" against the backdrop of a plain white set. If the characters' lines didn't exactly sparkle, their heavily made-up bodies—liberally doused in glitter and complemented with hair dyed in a variety of colors—did, providing the performance with its most enduring memory.

Compared to all this, Bowie's occasional live shows seemed woefully dull, at least to the visiting New Yorkers who caught him in action one night in north London. Wayne (later Jayne) County recalled: "We were so disappointed with him. We looked over at him and said, 'Just look at the folky old hippie!'" Bowie's "crime" was performing a largely acoustic show dressed in yellow bell-bottoms and a floppy hat. Nevertheless, the transatlantic Warhol obsessives duly bowed when Bowie introduced the visiting *Pork* cast from the stage, and Cherry Vanilla bared her breasts for the benefit of the sparse crowd.

When Tony Zanetta arranged a meeting with Warhol during Bowie's visit to New York a few weeks later, Warhol was typically reticent, choosing only to make conversation about Bowie's canary-yellow Anello & Davide shoes. He was reportedly less than impressed by David's recently penned musical tribute to him, leaving the room without saying a word as soon as it had finished. A cursory "great" on his return wasn't much of a confidence booster to Bowie. It was Warhol's favorite exclamation, and he had a habit of saying it in a way that made it sound like the most insincere compliment in the world.

Bowie hardly needed reminding that, however much an auteur could inflate himself by virtue of those who congregated around him, everything still depended on how convincing the persona of that enlarged personality was. When the detritus of New York life had begun to gravitate toward Warhol, the artist was already the most talked about creative talent of his generation. But when Bowie sought to place himself as the architect of an emerging scene at the me-and-my-friends show taped for

Radio 1 earlier that year, it was a scene fronted by a face few cared about. The failure of the closely related Arnold Corns project, where he first submerged his identity within a pseudonymous—and largely fictitious—group, served to confirm this lack of interest. That said, the short-lived Arnold Corns was the first flowering of the ideas that he had gleaned from Warhol.

In 1976, reflecting on his pre–*Ziggy Stardust* career, Bowie told Radio 1's Stuart Grundy that 1971 had been the year when he "got down to serious writing and [was] trying not to diversify too much." Prior to that, he added, he "would try and get involved in anything that I felt was a useful tool for an artistic medium, from writing songs to putting on art shows and street theater." In his own words, Bowie was "trying to be a one-man revolution." It's true that his arts lab at Beckenham had come and gone. So had the halfhearted attempts at a formal stage or screen career. But if there was ever a period when Bowie seriously began to think of himself as a one-man revolution, it was the summer of 1971.

Bowie, if not exactly waiting in the wings, ready to be called onto a beckoning stage, was at least beginning to lay foundations for a markedly different approach to rock stardom. With aspirations too grand to simply pass himself off as yet another rock 'n' roll hopeful, he began to adopt the Warholian guise of scene maker/master schemer. His little suburban arts lab experiment had failed miserably; spartan audiences would turn up (or not) to hear folk singer David Bowie strum his acoustic guitar and tell a few stories. His newfound support system of Angie, Defries, and Mick Ronson, though, gave him room to maneuver. He could step out of the role of the singleminded artist and become instead a creative nexus with several strings attached. Like Warhol before him, he envisaged designing, and ultimately lording over, a self-made microkingdom. The first step was to invent his own pop group and talk up his friends as future superstars.

The first of these potential superstars was a young, flamboyant stylist he'd met in the Sombrero, a predominantly gay club on the fashionable Kensington High Street. His name was Freddi Buretti, though Bowie, whose interests included art deco and twenties Hollywood glamor, chose to christen him Rudi Valentino in honor of the silent-screen idol. (The real Rudolph Valentino conformed closely to Bowie's tragic-hero ideal: Between 1921 and 1926 he was Hollywood's biggest box-office draw,

before being taken ill during a bout of publicity appearances and dying at the age of thirty-one, after complications arising from a gallstone attack.) Since returning from his first visit to America in February 1971, knowing that his Mercury/Philips contract would be up by June, Bowie had been making irregular visits to the (relatively cheap) studios at Radio Luxembourg and Underhill Studios in south London. By April, he was telling journalist George Tremlett that he hoped to produce albums by Rudi Valentino and Arnold Corns, predicting that Rudi would be the new Mick Jagger.

The only obvious fruits from this activity were two 45s that were credited to Arnold Corns and released by the tiny B&C label. The first paired two songs destined for the *Ziggy Stardust* album, "Moonage Daydream" and "Hang On to Yourself." The second, issued in 1972, revived "Hang On to Yourself," but was backed by another track, "Looking for a Friend." Both records sank without a trace. A fourth song from these sessions, "Man in the Middle," emerged in the mid-eighties, when the Arnold Corns tracks were collected on a Scandinavian twelve-inch release.

Compared with Bowie's previous single, "Holy Holy," which had been issued in January 1971 to the kind of silence that had been all too familiar in his career, the quartet of Arnold Corns songs were relaxed affairs. Bowie, so long afraid to dirty his hands with straight rock 'n' roll, had finally learned how to strut. Significantly, though, the choice of the pensive "Moonage Daydream" as the lead track on the first 45 showed the depth of his reserve. At this stage, the song owed more to the Beatles than New York: Its leaden percussion was straight out of the Ringo Starr school of drumming, hanging just behind the beat. And the bridge wasn't that far off from Paul McCartney's oompah-style piano-based material. What was most notable about the song, which is similar in structure to the eventual *Ziggy Stardust* version, were Bowie's vocals, which stayed in the upper registers, at times histrionically. It was a remarkable and highly stylized change from the impeccable sense of diction that had characterized so much of his earlier efforts.

If "Moonage Daydream" owed much to the British pop vernacular, "Hang On to Yourself" has always been seen as a shameless attempt to borrow the Velvet Underground sound. Bowie had picked up on *Loaded,* the Velvets' last album, during his first New York visit in February. One track, "Sweet Jane," was overtly plagiarized in "Hang On to Yourself," the line "And me I'm in a rock 'n' roll show" (later dropped from the *Ziggy Stardust* version) a direct steal from Reed's famous "And me I'm in a rock 'n' roll band."

It has been suggested that, prior to recording the song with Arnold Corns, Bowie intended it as a vehicle for Gene Vincent (like Vince Taylor, an out-of-favor leather boy). A version said to have been taped by the pair during Bowie's American promotional tour in February circulates among collectors. Frustratingly, there is no aural evidence of Vincent's involvement, just Bowie on acoustic, supported by handheld percussion and a wandering bass line. Even the backing vocals sound like a Bowie overdub.

The free-for-all sing-along "Looking for a Friend" also echoes the brighter mood that made *Loaded* the Velvet Underground's only pop album. This time, the vocals were handled by Bowie's would-be Mick Jagger figure, Rudi Valentino, whose ersatz Lou Reed monotone can also be heard on the extended-jaw strut of "Man in the Middle," the "Huh, he doesn't care at all" coming straight from the Reed songbook. But any Velvet Underground influence—whether latent or manifest—was underscored by Mick Ronson's Beck-like flourishes, most evident on "Man in the Middle," and a distinct country-rock influence on the breaks during "Looking for a Friend" and "Hang On to Yourself."

Though Arnold Corns was intended to include Runk, college-band pals of Freddi, there is no evidence that either bassist Polak de Somogyi or drummer Ralph St. Laurent Broadbent ever played on the recordings. Freddi Buretti and guitarist Mark Carr Pritchard have since been credit-

EMPIRE
LIVERPOOL

1st Performance 6-30
SUNDAY
JUNE   10

STALLS
£1·00
          87

THIS PORTION TO BE GIVEN UP

ed, but the Arnold Corns tracks are most notable for being the first to feature the trio of Mick Ronson, Woody Woodmandsey, and Trevor Bolder, soon to be the Spiders from Mars.

Bowie's starmaker role extended beyond the hapless Corns project. In April of 1971, he entered Trident Studios with singer (and another Sombrero Club regular) Sparky (alias Mickey) King to record "Rupert the Riley," produced by Bowie and engineered by Ken Scott. Billed as the Nick King All Stars, again to avoid contractual complications with Mercury/Philips, the pair also collaborated on David's "Miss Peculiar" (alias "How Lucky You Are"), with Sparky taking the lead vocals. Unlike Arnold Corns, who at least were immortalized on vinyl, nothing more was heard from the Nick King All Stars.

Now, six months before the sessions for *The Rise and Fall of Ziggy Stardust and the Spiders from Mars* began in earnest, the notion of Bowie fronting a flamboyantly clad, sexually ambiguous rock 'n' roll band was clearly back on the agenda. If Arnold Corns was always envisaged as a side project, an experiment in control and manipulation, the realization dawned that such a construction could be applied far more perfectly to himself. So by the end of the year, and with the basis for two albums in the bag, he decided to let public opinion hold sway.

MY DEATH WAITS . . .

AND THE CLOCK WAITS SO PATIENTLY
ON YOUR SONG.

—"Rock 'n' Roll Suicide," from
The Rise and Fall of Ziggy Stardust and the Spiders from Mars

I USED TO LIVE IN A ROOM FULL
OF MIRRORS
ALL I COULD SEE WAS ME
AND I TOOK MY SPIRIT AND I
SMASHED MY MIRROR
NOW THE WHOLE WORLD IS THERE
FOR ME TO SEE.

—"Room Full of Mirrors," from
***Rainbow Bridge*, Jimi Hendrix**

I'M DRAWN BETWEEN THE LIGHT
AND DARK.

—"Quicksand," from *Hunky Dory*

The Velvet Underground, Iggy Pop, Andy Warhol, *Pork,* even his own pro- totypical alter egos, pseudo-anonymity with the Hype and Arnold Corns: All were recent obsessions that conspired to tear holes in Bowie's sense of musical self-sufficiency. His Mod narcissism had always been tem- pered by self-doubt as he sought to justify his uniqueness by offering something that truly set him apart from and above his herdlike, fashion- following contemporaries. Even that narcissism was expressed in terms that suggested a flight from confused self, using idealized and tragic char- acters such as his half-brother Terry and Vince Taylor. The celebration of human collapse, found in the Velvet Underground's street-level minimal- ism, in Iggy Pop's bodily abuse, in the debauched meaninglessness of *Pork,* and in Warhol's mask-without-a-face persona, gave him the intel- lectual armor he'd been searching for. But it would be foolish to read these stepping-stones toward the self-obliterating, magnified antistardom that was *Ziggy Stardust* as an inevitable path.

The British pop netherworld Bowie continued to stalk was unlikely to embrace a dubious aesthetic plucked from a highly contentious corner of the New York art world. British pop stars were either "real" and truth seeking (John Lennon, Cat Stevens), "real" and romantic rock Lotharios (Ian Gillan, Robert Plant), or technical geniuses (Jimmy Page, Robert Fripp). Then there was a new breed of headline-grabbing idols, most notably Slade and T. Rex, who enraptured the post-Beatles audience in 1971 with a combination of simple rock 'n' roll hooks and eye-catching costumes. There was nothing more debilitating for a self-styled one-man revolutionary than having to clamber up someone else's greasy pole to instant celebrityhood. Instead, while soaking up the detritus of discarded (at least by rock's prevailing ideologies) musical and cultural traditions, Bowie continued to work within the compass of contemporary singer- songwriters.

The lethargy he had shown in the spring of 1970 during sessions for *The Man Who Sold the World* looks, on paper at least, to have precipitat- ed a crisis of songwriting confidence. Between the recording of that album and the release of *Hunky Dory* in December of 1971, Bowie released just two records under his own name, a rerecording of "Memory of a Free Festival" from his second solo album and "Holy Holy," backed by "All the Madmen" from *The Man Who Sold the World.* One new song spread across four sides was not encouraging.

David Bowie with Mick Ronson at Earls Court in 1973
BARRIE WENTZEL, COUR- TESY OF STAR FILE

He was still indecisive about whether or not to pursue the group format. In fact, such was Bowie's lack of commitment that Mick Ronson and
Mick "Woody" Woodmansey returned to Hull after work on *The Man Who
Sold the World* had been completed. They had a record deal, inked in
April 1970, as part of Angie's plan to raise funds to finance Bowie's
career. Benny Marshall, who'd played harmonica with the Hype on one or
two occasions, returned, and the trio was boosted by the addition of
bassist Trevor Bolder. The band's lone 45, "Fourth Hour of My Sleep" /
"Power of Darkness," issued in January 1971 on the Vertigo label, was
credited to Ronno. That wasn't surprising: Despite the vaguely anony-
mous blues-rock sound, Mick Ronson was clearly the band's leader. (In
fact, Ronson may have brought more to *The Man Who Sold the World*
than he's usually given credit for. "Early in Spring," one of two cuts recorded at a recently unearthed Rats session from the winter of 1969, turns out
to be the template for that album's proto-metal sound.)

Ronno, as Mick Ronson no doubt suspected, were taking a fast train
to nowhere, which is why he—together with Woodmansey and Bolder—
heeded Bowie's call in April 1971 to return to London and begin work on
his latest project. (Legend has it that bassist Rick Kemp was Ronson's first
choice, but that his balding head was deemed inappropriate.) The main
project, aside from sessions for Arnold Corns, was the *Hunky Dory* album.

If Ronson's handiwork can clearly be detected on the Arnold Corns
tracks, *Hunky Dory* suggests a different influence, confirmation that
Bowie was keeping his options open as late as mid-1971. The classically
trained Rick Wakeman, who'd previously worked with David on "Space
Oddity" and had since become one of the country's top keyboard ses-
sionmen, was the latest recruit in Bowie's roster of workmates.

"He invited me round to his flat in Beckenham, which I used to call
Beckenham Palace, and played me all these songs on his old twelve-
string," the pianist later recalled. "He told me to make as many notes as
I wanted. The songs were unbelievable, 'Changes,' 'Life On Mars,' one
after the other. He said he wanted to come at the album from a different
angle, that he wanted them to be based around the piano. So he told me
to play them as I would a piano piece, and that he'd then adapt everything
else around that. And that's what happened. We went into the studio and
I had total freedom to do whatever I liked throughout the album. Everyone

literally played around what I was playing. I still rate it as the finest collection of songs on one album."

Others, especially those in high places, agreed. Michael Watts in *Melody Maker* described *Hunky Dory* as "not only the best album Bowie has ever done, it's also the most inventive piece of songwriting to have appeared on record for a considerable time." The American magazine *Rock* called Bowie "the most singularly gifted artist creating music today. He has the genius to be to the 70's what Lennon, McCartney, Jagger and Dylan were to the 60's." To the *New York Times* he was "the most intellectually brilliant man yet to choose the long-playing album as his medium of expression."

Some of these assessments may be evidence of Defries' hype machine going into overdrive, but clearly a profound transformation had taken place in Bowie's work. Certainly, he had relocated his muse: Half of the songs on *Hunky Dory*—"Changes," "Oh! You Pretty Things," "Life on Mars," "Quicksand," "Andy Warhol," and "Queen Bitch"—remain, a quarter of a century later, on the Bowie A-list, evergreens as sophisticated as they are instantly memorable. The recruitment of Wakeman to transpose the songs to piano, giving them a classical luster more in keeping with rock's—or, more accurately, adult pop's—growing maturity, was a masterstroke. Less self-evident was the new discipline Bowie exercised in his writing.

His first solo album had woefully misread the direction in which the growing rock culture was moving; his second had been tainted by the expectations raised by "Space Oddity." *The Man Who Sold the World* had been a tripartite affair, with Visconti and Ronson calling many of the musical shots. *Hunky Dory* marked the return not only of Bowie the songwriter, but also of Bowie the keen—and more experienced—observer of musical trends. He'd watched as piano-based solo artists such as Elton John, Randy Newman, and Carole King had revitalized adult pop with intelligent yet accessible songwriting, technically adept but unencumbered by the increasingly tatty freak banner.

Hunky Dory gave Bowie a dignity that his previously erratic approach to songwriting had been unable to deliver. It bolstered his confidence, proving to his peers and those caught up in his star-seeking web that he was as capable a craftsman as any other recognition seeker. It also won him the record deal from which he hoped to launch a new career trajectory, a gamble that, should it come off, would bring him the only kind of stardom he desired.

For all its contra-rock singer-songwriterly tendencies, *Hunky Dory* contained, on a thematic level at least, many ideologically charged germs with which Bowie would help close one era and pry open another. Take the presentation of Bowie on the sleeve. Unlike his rock contemporaries, who'd begun to hide behind artfully designed record sleeves hinting at the far-flung conceptual nature of the music contained within, he was cast in unashamedly iconic terms, a throwback to the ambisexual appeal of the women from Hollywood's silent age. Like Greta Garbo on the prow of the ship at the end of *Queen Christina,* Bowie's tinted head was a suspended object of desire, his eyes languid, gazing out over his potential audience, away from the travails of the earthly humdrum and into a distant, unknown future. More than that, it was parody, a knowing embrace of an archaic kind of star system that thrived on the projection of superhuman ego archetypes. Of indeterminate sex, and with a gaze like that of the "sad-eyed merman" in his own song "The Supermen," Bowie had successfully projected himself in a way that his old Mod demeanor and his cross-dressing on the sleeve of *The Man Who Sold the World* had failed to do.

If he had always felt like an actor, as he has professed on countless occasions, Bowie was forever an aspiring one, seduced by those with infinitely better scripts: Terry, the family outcast, struggling to find a social role that would fit the one he had inside his head; Vince Taylor, the Elvis clone whose behavior on- and offstage conformed to the sense of separateness that Bowie reserved for icons of true star appeal; Jimi Hendrix and Syd Barrett, whose premature departures after offering brief glimpses of greatness only served to enhance their Otherness; and Andy Warhol, perhaps now his ultimate star, an empty vessel whose script was "you and me."

On *Hunky Dory,* Bowie (who referred to himself as "The Actor" on the sleeve) sidestepped his cast of antiheroes and began to prepare his manifesto of self-effacement and self-projection. And there was no clearer indication of this than the opening track, "Changes." In promotions for the album, Bowie gave his own track-by-track commentary, thumbnail sketches that clearly rooted the record in an era when meaning was all.

"This album is full of my changes and those of some of my friends," he wrote. But that comment belies the defining importance of "Changes" in Bowie's canon.

On a purely formal level, the constant shifts in tempo and key neatly mirror the song's meaning, aligning the concept of flux with a piece of music that's otherwise regularly structured. Lyrically, "Changes" is unashamedly autobiographical (like most singer-songwriters, Bowie "can't help thinking about me"), revisiting his past failures ("Every time I thought I'd got it made / It seemed the taste was not so sweet"), and looking forward to his newfound impenetrability (facing himself, he cannot see how "the others must see the faker," because he's "much too fast to take that test"). Detaching himself from those who "never leave the stream of warm impermanence," Bowie revisits his youth as one of the "children that you spit on / As they try to change their worlds," reminds himself of how that "strange fascination" continues to excite him, before firing an important warning shot, "Look out you rock 'n' rollers!"

There is scant evidence on *Hunky Dory* that rock 'n' rollers would have had something to fear. When it comes, by way of the penultimate track on the album, the song is so out of place it appears to be the joker in the pack. Titled "Queen Bitch," the track is hung on a staccato Mick Ronson chord progression that sounds like "Sweet Jane" in reverse, while Bowie's voice alternates from a Lou Reed drawl to choruses that resemble the cast of *Pork* having an almighty backstage fight. Inspired by Bowie's visits to Warhol's Factory, "Queen Bitch" is the song on which Bowie's career pivoted, where his Arnold Corns alter ego popped out as if a lid had just been opened on this jack-in-the-box. Rick Wakeman's delicate piano trills were nowhere to be heard.

It was the rest of *Hunky Dory* that was a red herring in terms of Bowie's subsequent musical development. "Oh! You Pretty Things" again revisited the McCartney school of piano/bass unison playing; "Life On Mars" was almost classical in its execution, even though Bowie conceived it as his own take on Sinatra's "My Way"; "Kooks," written in honor of his newborn son, Zowie, was a suitably childlike spin on easy listening, a naïveté also mined on his cover of Biff Rose's "Fill Your Heart."

The album would have been given a quite different complexion had "Fill Your Heart," which opened the second side, not replaced a Bowie original at the last minute. "Bombers," previewed on Radio 1 in June, revived the apocalyptic vision first visited on "We Are Hungry Men" on his 1967 album. Although the specter of nuclear disaster had subsided since the early sixties, Bowie still lived in its shadow, though he seemed to view any impending A-bomb inferno with a comic edge. "Think we're in for a big surprise / Right between the eyes" was hardly "We Shall Overcome"; neither was the spectacle of the old man who took the brunt of the explosion "floating high up in the sky."

Two of the most angst-filled tracks on the album, "Quicksand" and "The Bewlay Brothers," resembled the dark, confessional atmosphere that underpinned much of *The Man Who Sold the World*. The longest songs on the record, they dealt with themes that had preoccupied Bowie for several years, and which were now reaching a kind of exorcism. It's little wonder that Bowie was drawn to Aleister Crowley's search for higher spiritual planes, distilled with a little Nietzsche on "Quicksand," which concludes that he's "just a mortal with potential of a Superman." Tiring of living on the pointed horns of a dilemma, of "sinking in the quicksand of my thought," Bowie's dialogue with himself reaches another impasse in the final stanza: "Knowledge comes with death's release."

"The Bewlay Brothers," which Bowie misleadingly characterized in the *Hunky Dory* promotion as "*Star Trek* in a leather jacket," had nothing to do with extraterrestrials and everything to do with figures of mystification here on earth, namely his half-brother Terry. The title, a thinly disguised reference to David and Terry's relationship, was at least as baffling as its subject, which, in its more grounded moments, portrayed the pair waltzing through a world that owed more to Tolkien than the green and pleasant land of England. Part farewell (Terry rarely appeared in a Bowie song again), the song was also in part a merging of characters ("he's chameleon, comedian, Corinthian and caricature"), as Bowie's idealized projection of the antihero began to consume the vacuum where his own sense of self, now intellectually abandoned, had once been.

More than anything else, the obvious commercial and creative power of the songs on *Hunky Dory* fattened up Bowie as a marketable commodity to prospective record company bidders. The Mercury deal was over in June of 1971, and it was clear that they were not happy with Bowie's image or with the sales figures of *The Man Who Sold the World*. Having ex–Herman's Hermits vocalist Peter Noone cover "Oh! You Pretty Things"—which reached No. 12 on the U.K. charts—confirmed Bowie's potential not only as a soloist but as a songwriter capable of success. Finding the right record company, the one that would make enough money available for Defries to get into a huge marketing campaign, was a necessary step if everything was indeed to be hunky dory with Bowie's career.

RCA Records—once the all-powerful Radio Corporation of America—had fallen on hard times in its attempts to keep abreast of the vicissitudes of pop. Signing Elvis Presley in 1955 had been a gamble that had paid off handsomely, but there was a downside to having a roster headed by the most lucrative name in popular music. The company spent much of the Presley proceeds on developing stereo sound and watched helplessly as other labels made more astute signings in a pop market that RCA had presumed would soon go away. In the late sixties, the label enjoyed a two-year renaissance with the Monkees and a token underground act, Jefferson Airplane. But by 1971, the stable was desperately in need of an overhaul. To that effect, RCA signed the Velvet Underground's Lou Reed as a soloist, and the Kinks, under the auspices of new A&R director Dennis Katz, whose job it was to revamp the company's music division.

Seduced by an acetate of *Hunky Dory* and some smooth-talking spiel about how Bowie was destined to become the Elvis Presley of the seventies, Katz took the bait and signed Bowie. The fact that Defries asked for a modest advance of $37,500 per LP provided an added attraction. The manager knew exactly what he was doing: He made sure that RCA would pick up the tab for promoting Bowie, and that Defries's management company, Gem, would retain outright ownership of the master tapes.

THE SONGS

Sessions for *The Rise and Fall of Ziggy Stardust and the Spiders from Mars* began weeks before *Hunky Dory* even hit the shops. That was unusual by the standards of the rock era, especially in the early seventies, when a lengthy period of preparation was an integral part of the great rock charade as it strived to concoct ever more grandiloquent musical statements. Quick turnover in the studio was conducive to "manufactured" pop, but it had no place in the art of the rock album.

Several factors were involved in Bowie's hasty return to the studio. With the trusted missus and manager there to protect, market, and make decisions for him, at least on the business and social levels, he had been free to become a full-time, pleasantly pampered creative artist without having to agonize about Ken Pitt's latest decision-making folly or selling his soul to the record company executive nursing a drink at the bar. Bowie had been stockpiling songs during the past eighteen months; some, including "Lightning Frightening," the resurrected "Tired of My Life," the Kurt Weill-ish "How Lucky You Are," a version of Jacques Brel's "Port of Amsterdam," "Rupert the Riley" (a rather silly tribute to his battered car), and "Bombers," were belatedly released. Only the Brel cover played any real role in his new career, forming a regular part of the early Ziggy live set.

Yet, apart from the two Arnold Corns versions, just two stripped-down home demos of songs from *Ziggy Stardust* have ever officially been made public, suggesting that much of the album was hastily written, probably during the summer and early autumn months of 1971, and largely inspired by the prospect of securing the RCA deal (duly made in

David Bowie and the Spiders from Mars on the set of the "Jean Genie" promo film, November 1972 ©1972, 1996 MICK ROCK, COURTESY OF STAR FILE

September). (In fact, Bowie has said that *Ziggy Stardust* was the only LP where he'd gone into the studio "armed with proper songs.") But the biggest spur of all was probably the sustained success of Bowie's fellow lapsed Mod, Marc Bolan.

Around the time the *Ziggy Stardust* sessions began in earnest, Bolan, with his newly abbreviated band T. Rex, was enjoying his third hit of the year and surfing the tide of what the press had dubbed "T. Rextasy." For all Bowie's talk of change, and warnings that rock 'n' rollers ought to be on the lookout, it was Bolan who had first effected an unlikely and groundbreaking transformation from last outpost of underground idealism into pop icon. He did this by realigning his music with fifties rock 'n' roll, and remaking his image in a sparkling style that owed as much to vintage Hollywood as it did to multicolored hippie costumes.

Shaking off any post-Beatles malaise, pop had begun to steamroll once more. Throughout 1970, the British singles charts had been the preserve of a host of fly-by-night groups—vehicles for formula-driven songwriters and fronted by a series of drab session musicians. Bolan's defection from the security of the beard-stroking margins made pop a national interest once more. It had become a terrain worth fighting for, and fellow stray cats like Rod Stewart and Elton John moved quickly to grab a piece of the action. To say that Bowie, the biggest underachiever of the lot, had sensed his time had come might be a cliché writ large. But let's face it, a resurgence of public yearning for flamboyant, larger-than-life stars, and a return to the basic ingredients of rock 'n' roll (economical songwriting, four-piece groups singing about that old bump and grind, a dream-drenched teenage audience ripe for seduction)—Bowie couldn't have engineered a more perfect set of circumstances if he'd been handed a wand.

The *Ziggy Stardust* sessions took place at Trident Studios in central London, which, with Advision and Olympic, was one of the top three independent studios in Britain. It was familiar ground: Bowie had recorded much of *The Man Who Sold the World* and all of *Hunky Dory* there. With him was Ken Scott, a safe pair of hands who had done his training alongside George Martin with the Beatles at Abbey Road and had engineered Bowie's 1969 album and *The Man Who Sold the World* before being promoted to the role of producer for *Hunky Dory.* This time, he shared the production credits with the artist.

Bowie has since remarked that Scott was "sort of my George Martin, in a way." That could mean many things, from guide and mentor to someone who could mold himself to the singer's requirements. The latter scenario is more likely. "George very much left the Beatles to do their own thing," says Scott, "which is exactly what I did with David. He had all the musical ideas he needed. I've always considered the job of producer as one of getting across the best possible performance from the artist in the way that the artist wants it." For Scott, the main requirement was keeping one step ahead of Bowie, particularly because they were still working with eight-track equipment (the norm was sixteen by this point). "David wasn't particularly good at explaining exactly what he wanted, so you had to be economical with the production in case he said he wanted a one hundred twenty five-piece orchestra. Let's call it translation."

Happily for Scott, this time there was little call for the number of arrangements that had been necessary for the *Hunky Dory* material. "That album was coherent in that each song was treated specifically in accordance to its needs. On *Ziggy Stardust,* the basics were virtually the same for all the tracks. It was only the nuances in each song that would vary." Despite Bowie's insistence to Scott at the start of the sessions that "you're not going to like this album, it's much more rock 'n' roll" (a suggestion Scott still finds baffling), there was no discussion either of any Ziggy concept or of the kind of sound Bowie was looking for prior to recording. "I knew nothing of the Arnold Corns songs," insists Scott.

"The sessions weren't very much different to any of the other Bowie sessions," he maintains. "We recorded quickly, just as we always did. It was very much a band feel, with all the members laying down their basic tracks, patching them up to eliminate any mistakes, and then adding the overdubs. The bassist and drummer weren't around much for that part of it. But Mick Ronson was important. Like me, he had the job of trying to anticipate what David wanted, and then translating that into musical terms. In that respect he was very good. They were both on the same wavelength. He knew exactly what David wanted at that time."

Surprisingly, especially from today's perspective where artists tend to have almost total control over every aspect of the recording process, Bowie and Ronson rarely sat in on mixing sessions, where the sound of the album could have been altered considerably. "That was done on trust," says Scott. "And that wasn't unusual then. The only time I ever saw

David at that part of the process was for a couple of tracks on *Pin Ups* [1973]."

Despite bringing an armful of songs into the studio with him, at first Bowie was unclear about the concept and the actual track selection for the finished product. "It Ain't Easy" had been taped back in September and had been in the running for inclusion on *Hunky Dory*. "Star" (originally titled "Rock 'n' Roll Star"), "Hang On to Yourself," "Moonage Daydream," "Soul Love," and "Lady Stardust," together with the later discarded "Sweet Head," were recorded during the first two weeks of November. By 15 December 1971, a master tape had been made with "Five Years," "Soul Love," "Moonage Daydream," "Round and Round" (by Chuck Berry), and "Port of Amsterdam" (by Jacques Brel) on side one and "Hang On to Yourself," "Ziggy Stardust," "Velvet Goldmine," a rerecording of "Holy Holy," "Star," and "Lady Stardust" on side two.

Had the album been released in this form, ending with "Lady Stardust" finding success rather than suicide, there would have been no rise and fall, perhaps even no Ziggy Stardust beyond the song that bore his name. In fact, at the end of 1971, the album was provisionally billed as *Round and Round;* if anything; perhaps a comment on the cyclical nature of the pop merry-go-round.

This order was soon scrapped, and in January the band returned to the studios to record three more tracks: "Rock 'n' Roll Suicide," "Suffragette City," and "Starman." Ken Scott has vivid memories of recording "Starman" at a separate session from the other two songs. "I think there may have been input from Mainman [the management company formed by Defries]," he says. "It had something to do with there being no obvious single on the album." A second master tape, dated 2 February 1972, conformed to the eventual finished track order with one exception: "Round and Round" was later replaced by "Starman."

In January, Bowie had also discussed his forthcoming album by phone from London with an American radio station. This marked the only occasion when he talked about the recording of the *Ziggy Stardust* album in detail. The conversation is revealing for its insights into the status of individual tracks and for laying bare the lack of any real musical coherence behind the so-called Ziggy concept, especially in its early stages. He confirmed that "Bombers" ("a kind of skit on Neil Young!") and "It Ain't Easy" had been dropped from *Hunky Dory,* and that an acoustic "Port of

Amsterdam," "Velvet Goldmine" (then titled "He's a Goldmine" and described as "a lovely tune, but probably a little provocative"), and a new version of "Holy Holy" had indeed formed part of the *Ziggy Stardust* sessions. But his explanation of why "Round and Round" was dropped opened a window on the album's key idea, that of a fictional Ziggy and the Spiders inhabiting a real rock 'n' roll band. "It would have been the kind of number that Ziggy would have done onstage. He jammed it for old times' sake in the studio, and our enthusiasm for it probably waned after we heard it a few times. We replaced it with a thing called 'Starman.' I don't think it's any great loss, really."

During the golden age of the concept album, roughly from 1968 to 1975, this predictable by-product of rock's newfound self-importance came in two configurations. One, in which a clear narrative unfolds during the course of a lengthy song cycle, was closely related to opera. The most obvious examples of what was dubbed rock opera were *Tommy,* which eventually found its rightful place on the stage; and *Jesus Christ Superstar,* which was designed as a stage show with a tie-in album from the start. Rather less open to ridicule was the concept album that shunned the narrative format in favor of building a record around a more general theme. By far the best-known example is Pink Floyd's summer of '73 opus, *The Dark Side of the Moon,* written largely by bassist Roger Waters, another renegade from the days of hippie idealism. Waters took a long, cool look at the world around him and built the entire epic on his observations, describing greed, war, corruption, and spiritual emptiness. It was either the work of a hopeless misanthrope or a brilliantly clear insight into the workings of the world, depending on which side of the fence you sat.

Judged by its title alone, *The Rise and Fall of Ziggy Stardust and the Spiders from Mars* should have been the rock opera to end all rock operas. Never mind *Jesus Christ Superstar;* this was the archetypal Rise and Fall as it applied to the pop world, a world that in recent months had experienced a genuine sense of loss with the breakup of the Beatles, and with them, the cheery innocence that had made the sixties go "pop." By building into the title the chimera of a narrative concept, Bowie was able to intrigue audiences accustomed to thought-provoking music, and for those new to such sophistication, Ziggy's rise and fall was an invitation into something esoteric and daring, even if they couldn't quite grasp its wider meaning. Bowie could, but he remained artfully hesitant when it came to stringing together an actual narrative. He told his airwave inquistor:

> It wasn't really started as a concept album. It got kind of broken up because I found other songs that I wanted to put in the album that wouldn't fit in with the story of Ziggy. So at the moment it's a little fractured and a little fragmented.
>
> What you have on that album when it finally comes out is a story which doesn't really take place. It's just a few little scenes from the life of a band called Ziggy Stardust and the Spiders from Mars, who could feasibly be the last band on earth, because we're living the last five years of Earth.
>
> I'm not at all certain, because I wrote it in such a way that I just got the numbers into the album in any order that they cropped up. . . . It depends which state you listen to it in. Once I've written an album, my interpretations of the numbers on it are totally different afterwards than when I wrote them. And I find that I learn a lot from my own albums about me.

One suspects that Bowie already knew that *The Rise and Fall of Ziggy Stardust and the Spiders from Mars* would provide the lesson he'd been waiting for, the one that would finally liberate him from his struggles with identity and supply him with the mask with which he could enter into the netherworld of celebrity. (Of course, it only served to intensify those difficulties.)

Bowie's self-analysis might seem to obscure the humdrum reality of turning up at Trident at two in the afternoon on a cold winter's day in gloomy London to spend the best part of his waking hours creating a suitable set of songs for his fifth LP. But music was merely the springboard, the key social process for his generation, offering the potential for self-transcendence, a headlong dive into the Other. The songs on *Ziggy Stardust* are vaguely themed, three-minute bites with a clear appeal to pop and rock audiences alike. Taken collectively, they suggest something of far greater importance than the mere details of musical style. The full ramifications of this would be brought more clearly into focus with the addition of the Bowie/Ziggy persona, which manifested itself in interviews, through advertisements, and, most significantly, via the concert platform. But Ziggy couldn't exist if he had no songs to sing.

Living on the precipice of an impending apocalypse. Projecting an ego ideal in the manner of Dr. Frankenstein's creation. Exposing the nature of the medium, in the manner of Brecht or Warhol. Alluding to the ephemeral nature of pop ("We've got five years / That's all we've got"). These themes, which have been addressed by Bowie with varying degrees of sophistication throughout his career, are explored in the album's opening song, delivered in a manner that starts out like reportage but finishes up as a declamatory cry for help.

Like so much of his earlier work, there's a cinematic quality to "Five Years." The pensive start, ushered in with a walking-pace drumbeat, captures the sense of the narrator-as-journalist surveying scenes of imminent earthly destruction (an acutely real prospect in Bowie's crisis-filled head). The oppositions that fueled his creative energies—self/other, life/death, rise/fall—build into a subtext ("fat"/"slim," "nobody"/"somebody," "short"/"tall"), as does the sense that the star figure cannot exist without audience or acolytes: "never thought I'd need so many people."

Almost as a harbinger of the forthcoming cataclysm, Bowie works psychological breakdown ("A girl my age went off her head") and the ruination of childhood innocence ("Hit some tiny children") into his deathly scenario. This couplet has its origins in "Shadow Man," first demoed at Haddon Hall in May 1970 (as "The Man"), and reworked at Trident in April 1971 before being cut with the Spiders at the September 1971 *Ziggy Stardust* sessions. With its references to the Shadow Man being "really you," how you "Look in his eyes and see your reflection," "Shadow Man" presages the blurred relationship between Bowie and the Ziggy character.

"Five Years" further muddies the crucial juxtaposition of David Bowie the performer and Ziggy, his creation. Into scenes of despair, prompted by the news of an imminent holocaust, steps the idealized figure of Ziggy, "looking so fine" and blissfully unaware that he was "in this song." The distance between the songwriter and his fictional construct is undercut in the next line, with the first-person reference to feeling "like an actor," which in turn gives way to the climactic line, "I kiss you, you're beautiful, I want you to walk," the suggestion being that this is a sort of Dr. Frankenstein, or better still Dr. Jekyll, masquerading as his own creation. While he basked in a Warholian world of personality creation, Bowie would also have been well aware that in releasing such forces, the threat, and perhaps the perverse thrill, of self-destruction wasn't too far away.

Co-producer Ken Scott recalls that Bowie did the vocal in two takes, a technical maneuver that mirrored the singer/character's metaphorical split in personality. "The vocal range was quite different for the second half of the song, and so we had to adjust the levels to compensate for that," he says.

"Five Years" was one of the first *Ziggy* songs to be granted a national platform when it was performed on *The Old Grey Whistle Test,* televised early in February 1972. It remained a staple of Bowie's live set from 1972 through 1978.

"Soul Love"

"Five Years" provided the album's cultural backdrop and introduced the Ziggy character. But attempting to tease out any clear narrative from much of the rest of the album is difficult: As Bowie told his radio interviewer, on a purely narrative level, the album is fragmented to the point of incoherence.

Despite the assertion of the Gillmans, who claim in their book *Alias David Bowie* that the song is Ziggy's soliloquy on love and sex, "Soul Love" is probably one of those tracks that Bowie just happened to have around at the time and couldn't resist slotting into the set. Its gentle calm, with childlike single-note backing vocals ("mainly David," says Scott, "though sometimes Ronno joined in") straight out of the first T. Rex album, is deceptive, for what might appear to be a simple love song is riddled with cynicism. "Love descends on those defenseless"; it is blind, idiotic, and the province of the false god-worshipping "priest that tastes the word." The Fall is everywhere: The song recognizes only "stone love," the love for a corpse illustrated by the image of a mother kneeling beside the grave of her son, "who gave his life to save the slogan." Love is defined not by peaceable coexistence but by war.

Just as there was no place for the myth of romantic love on the *Ziggy Stardust* album, neither was there much room for "Soul Love" in the Ziggy stage shows during 1972 and 1973—the song was performed only on selected dates during the 1973 American tour, most notably at the two New York shows in February. Bowie briefly resurrected "Soul Love" for his 1978 world tour (a live version can be found on *Stage*), while Mick Ronson recorded it in the mid-seventies for his abandoned third solo album.

"Moonage Daydream"

At the famous Santa Monica performance in October 1972, midway through Bowie's first American tour, he introduced "Moonage Daydream" as "a song written by Ziggy." Despite its origins as an Arnold Corns side, it was recast as a "Ziggy" song within a Bowie album, a change underscored by drastically reworked lyrics.

As the curtains are raised with two bursts of stop-start power chords, Bowie-as-Ziggy announces the arrival of the extraterrestrial rock 'n' roll animal: "I'm an alligator . . . I'm the space invader, I'll be a rock 'n' rollin' bitch for you." Ziggy's alien status is sustained with the use of such terms as "ray-gun," "space face," and the song's oft-repeated title. This is enhanced by Bowie's heavily reverbed vocals, metallic power chords interspersed with some soaring guitar riding high on sustain, and the fluttering of cosmic keyboard sounds lurking just beneath the surface. Bowie's "far out!" during the break recasts an underground cliché as extraterrestrial-speak.

He also used the break to pay homage to a record from his youth. "That was David's idea," says Scott of the unison playing of a baritone sax and what was either a flute or a piccolo. "He'd heard it on an old Coasters record, loved the sound, and made it clear that was what he wanted." Bowie had no knowledge of the phased strings at the end of the song: They were added by Ken Scott during the mixing stage.

Unsurprisingly, given its central role on the album, "Moonage Daydream" was a permanent fixture of Bowie's shows between 1971 and 1974 and can be found in live form on *Ziggy Stardust: The Motion Picture* and *David Live*.

"Starman"

If "Moonage Daydream" heralds the first real stirring of space invader Ziggy, then "Starman" is the song that put Bowie and his fellow travelers in the shop window. It delivers his creation to a wider audience, both in terms of the loosely unfolding narrative on the LP, and as the album's— and therefore Bowie/Ziggy's—flagship single. "Starman" heralded Bowie's return to the singles chart for the first time in almost three years, giving chart watchers the impression that the now two-hit wonder specialized only in space-related songs.

The song's opening—a distant voice humming incoherently over gently strummed acoustic chords—accentuated the feeling that "Starman" was indeed the son of "Space Oddity." There was no overt mention of Ziggy, just a vague sense that Major Tom had been reborn as a rock 'n' roller about to "blow our minds."

The sense of déjà vu was magnified by the appropriation of a few musical tricks from other songs. The chorus, as Bowie has acknowledged, was lifted from "Over the Rainbow," the *Wizard of Oz* song in which young Judy Garland dreams of a distant utopia far away from her troubled life in rural America. The song also quotes the Supremes' "You Keep Me Hangin' On" with the guitar/piano morse-code effect just before the chorus (also used by Blue Mink in their 1969 hit "Melting Pot"), and, after Bowie gives Bolan a nod with "Let all the children booh-geh!," it borrows from Dave Edmunds's 1970 rock-a-boogie chart topper "I Hear You Knockin'."

Placed in the context of the record, "Starman" echoes the sense of an unfolding media event hinted at on "Five Years": Bowie, or the narrator, first hears the Starman on his radio; he switches on the television to see if he can find him there too, but it is by telephone that he confirms the news of his arrival. References to "the children" suggest that the Starman has come to liberate the young at heart.

Bowie quickly tired of "Starman," and it was dropped from the Ziggy shows by the summer of 1973.

"It Ain't Easy"

Always regarded as the red herring on *Ziggy Stardust,* this cover version was recorded in the summer of 1971, with a view to possible inclusion on *Hunky Dory.* In keeping with the predominant style of those sessions, it is more piano-based and singer-songwriterly in its delivery than the declamatory style that characterizes so much of *Ziggy Stardust.* And the slide guitar roots it in the warmer, mid-1971 manner of Arnold Corns.

With so many of his own songs at his disposal, it is baffling that Bowie chose to include this number by the little-known American song-writer Ron Davies (no relation to the Kinks' Ray Davies, who on several occasions has been miscredited with writing the song). Considering the appearance of Biff Rose's "Fill Your Heart" on *Hunky Dory*, perhaps Bowie was motivated by a need to champion the occasional diamond underdog, though "It Ain't Easy" wasn't entirely unknown in the U.K.— Long John Baldry had covered it in 1971, and it was also available on Ron Davies's album *Silent Songs Through the Land.* There are also unsubstantiated rumors that the Rats once covered the song, suggesting that Bowie may have been introduced to it by Mick Ronson. Bowie has ignored the track ever since.

According to Ken Scott, Dana Gillespie helped out on backing vocals.

"Lady Stardust"

Apparently first demoed at Haddon Hall in spring 1971 as "He Was Alright (The Band Was All Together)," "Lady Stardust" is another piano-led song. In emphasizing the "feminine" side of the Stardust persona, it is far more in keeping with the album's central motif of debauched celebrity than the preceding track.

Ziggy personified several themes taken from Bowie's own life, not least the projection of his own narcissistic fantasies onto other cult figures. But "Lady Stardust" is the first of three songs on the album that have prompted a quest to pinpoint their true inspiration. The most notable clue for this track was put forward by Bowie himself during two concerts at the Rainbow Theatre, London, in August 1972. In these rare performances of the song, which was used to open the shows, Marc Bolan's face was projected onto a screen.

Taking the lyrics at face value, there was no doubt that people would have pointed to Bolan; he was, after all, the man who introduced the world to glam rock, wore foundation on his face, fake teardrops under his eyes, and glitter on his cheeks. This accentuated his androgynous features, as did his "long black hair, his animal grace." But Bolan's songs of "darkness and disgrace/dismay"? You'd be hard pressed to find evidence of these on "Ride a White Swan" or "Hot Love."

It is inevitable that Bowie would have taken elements of his arche-typal rock star from Bolan. The pair had engaged in mutual appreciation and rivalry for several years, ever since they'd hung around the bars on Denmark Street in the mid-sixties hoping that someone important would notice them. By spring 1971, when Bowie was apparently writing "Lady Stardust," Bolan was already being acclaimed as the first pop star of the seventies. If it was a tribute to his rival, "Lady Stardust" is appropriately bit-tersweet, the "He was alright" refrain being delicately undercut by a minor-chord melancholy, not to mention Bowie's confession that he "smiled sadly for a love I could not obey." A fellow struggler now basking in newfound celebrity wouldn't have received an unconditional blessing from Bowie, but he would have made that goal seem all the more attainable.

"Star"

"Lady Stardust" delivered Ziggy to his audience. "Star" ventures into the mind of a boy in the crowd, daydreaming about how he might also "make a transformation as a rock 'n' roll star."

Even if his later suggestion that most listeners do not pay attention to lyrics as much as songwriters imagine they do is correct, few by now could have missed the central theme running through the album; help-fully, the word "star" had been incorporated into the titles of three of the songs. And this time the manifesto was laid bare: This new star—Bowie, Ziggy, maybe even you or me—was not God given, like the stars of old. He was a construct, someone who didn't want to fight on the streets of Belfast or stay at home on the dole. Someone who, like Labor politician and architect of the National Health Service Nye Bevan, "tried to change the nation," or like "Sonny," who wanted to "turn the world." Or, of course, like the ultimate subterranean iconoclast, David Bowie, who, to the relentless drive of a Velvet Underground–style backing track, was "so wiped out by things as they are." "Star" encapsulates Bowie's rock 'n' roll fantasy. With fame, money, and affection, he "could fall asleep at night as a rock 'n' roll star."

Being one of the more upbeat tracks on the album, it is surprising that "Star" never made it onto Ziggy-era set lists. The song was introduced in 1978, and it later appeared on *Stage,* the document of that year's world tour. The song was given even greater prominence in 1983 when it opened the "Serious Moonlight" tour where, segued with "The Jean Genie," it provided a nostalgic entrée for the radically redesigned star.

Propelled by a three-chord trick that was part Velvet Underground, part Eddie Cochran, "Hang On to Yourself" was deemed sufficiently electric to open the majority of Ziggy shows through 1972 and 1973. But in its studio form, Bowie's acoustic guitar is at least as prominent as Mick Ronson's electric, and Ronno even throws in a country-rock slide solo during the break. That said, this recording was still a marked intensification of the sluggish Arnold Corns version taped several months earlier. The single verse used for that prototype was now ditched in favor of two newly written verses that dealt with groupies, the rock 'n' roll lifestyle, and Ziggy's backing band, the Spiders from Mars. Lyrically slight, "Hang On to Yourself" is most notable for its chorus refrain, which amounts to a warning about the dangers of stardom (and masturbation): "If you think we're gonna make it / You better hang on to yourself."

"Hang On to Yourself," a regular in the Ziggy live set, was revived for the 1978 tour. Live versions can be found on *Ziggy Stardust: The Motion Picture* and *Stage*.

The nearest thing to a title track, "Ziggy Stardust" is the key conceptual track on the album, pinning down the sense of masquerade through the words of an eyewitness intimate (who may or may not be one of the Spiders), while at the same time bringing the Ziggy character to life with a series of loaded references. These preserve the mystery of Ziggy's identity, the search for which was in a way a fruitless quest but nevertheless fun, providing the album with a talking point to preoccupy critics and the public alike. "He played it left hand"—that had to be Jimi Hendrix. "He was the Nazz"—well, both Alice Cooper and Todd Rundgren used to front bands called the Nazz, and let's not forget the world's leading Nazarene and enduring cult idol, Jesus Christ. "Making love with his ego"—Jim Morrison, surely. "With God-given ass"—Mick Jagger, perhaps, or Iggy Pop, who by now was being managed by Defries. "Well-hung and snow-white tan"? Well, they all claimed to be that one.

Less obvious inspirations included a tailor's shop called Ziggy's, which Bowie is said to have spotted while traveling on a train, and the Legendary Stardust Cowboy, like Tiny Tim, a veteran of *Rowan & Martin's Laugh-In*. But while Tiny was well aware of the novelty value of his appearances, the not-so-legendary country performer was apparently mortified to discover that he was booked only for laughs. Bowie has since described the work of the singer, who once recorded a song titled "I Took a Trip on a Gemini Spacecraft," as "the most anarchistic, nihilistic stuff you've ever heard in your life."

Other possible sources of inspiration were the early writings of pop mythologist Nik Cohn. His novel *I Am Still the Greatest Says Johnny Angelo,* published in 1967, charted the rise and fall of a pulp hero, "A legend, the legend of Johnny Angelo, the story of what he was and what he dreamed he was." Steeped in pop mythology, the book contains many of the elements that had similarly excited Bowie: dreams of future heroism, style obsession, incomparable fame, and the gaudy allure of tragedy, as Johnny commits murder and is finally gunned down by the police. In the words of one of Angelo's acolytes, Arthur: "Violence and glamour and speed, splendour and vulgarity, danger and gesture and style—these were the things that he valued, nothing else."

The quest to locate the "authentic" Ziggy was always going to prove futile. Ziggy, the "leper messiah," was so obviously a composite culled from a long list of rock 'n' roll heroes and miscreants (preferably both), many real, some imagined. All these elements were distilled to create an object that conformed to Bowie's own idea of the perfect star: untouchable, unknowable, and on course for a tragic end. Someone who "took it all too far," who was taken to the abyss by virtue of his own fame. Bowie, desperate for control and yet just as desperate to experience what it felt like to be out of control, hardly had a death wish. But to create, and perhaps act out, the part of a character who did was the role he'd been waiting for. And in "Ziggy Stardust," he had finally achieved it.

"Suffragette City"

One of the final tracks to be recorded for the album, "Suffragette City" is a relentless slice of glammed-up rock 'n' roll, an urgent and resoundingly streetwise companion to the bedroom fantasies of "Star." It is rock 'n' roll, but without those lumbering sevenths that have sustained pub bands for almost half a century. Instead, Ronson played the chords straight, giving the song an added urgency and abrasiveness—a trick already well practiced by the vanguard of subterranean American rock, the Velvet Underground and the Stooges. Suitably unadorned, this brutality was enhanced by the unremitting piano, which was straight out of John Cale's artfully rudimentary playing on the Velvets' "White Light/White Heat."

"Suffragette City" has little to do with the Ziggy narrative; instead, it continues where "Hang On to Yourself" leaves off, a slice of rock 'n' roll lifestyle festooned with "mellow thighed chicks" to add to the notches already left by the "funky thigh collectors" of the earlier song. Lyrically, its appeal is all in the title, a vogueish nod to the feminist movement that grew up with the counterculture, which probably doubled as an invitation to a mystifying futuristic scenario.

It was impossible to listen to the urban rush of "Suffragette City" in the summer of 1972, especially in the wake of the *Clockwork Orange*–inspired panic over mugging, without imagining that cities were places where only the strong could survive. Anyone in doubt would have noted Bowie's reference to the "Droogies," the havoc-wreaking gang in the film whose antics caused headaches for the British Board of Film Censors and for Anthony Burgess, the author of the book on which the film was based. Even the climactic "Wham bam, thank you Ma'am!", a late sixties Small Faces single (and a phrase later used by American rock journalist Lester Bangs), could be construed as a reference to bag-snatching, though quickie sex was the more likely inspiration.

The heavy sax sound that adds another layer of sleaze to the backing was, according to Ken Scott, not played by a honking, sweat-drenched sax section at all, but by an ARP synthesizer. "David had this idea for a big sax sound, bigger than anything he could play, so we hooked up this huge synth, fiddled around until we got the closest sound to a sax as possible, and left Mick Ronson to play the right notes."

"Suffragette City" quickly became one of the best-known songs on *Ziggy Stardust,* not least because it was coupled with "Starman" on the original 45, thus making it a staple of pub jukeboxes. (A live version also played B-side to "Young Americans" in 1975.) It was performed on every David Bowie tour between 1972 and 1978, made an appearance on all three live albums, and was issued as a single in 1976 to promote the *Changesonebowie* collection.

If "Suffragette City" pointed toward a hyperelectric rock 'n' roll future, "Rock 'n' Roll Suicide" suggested the opposite. Ziggy's five years were up. His rise had been followed by that most perfect fall. He'd bowed out while at the peak of his powers. But was it suicide? The brakes certainly snarled as he stumbled down the road, reviving memories of the road-crash route to rock 'n' roll heaven (Eddie Cochran, Johnny Kidd, and James Dean). Or perhaps it was simply a case of succumbing to the abyss of mental torture that celebrity wreaks on its most gifted, most romantically charged, most sensitive souls. With Ziggy's "head all tangled up" as the "knives seem to lacerate [his] brain," that does appear to be the likely scenario.

In the album's final act, as the song shifts from its rock 'n' roll–ballad chord progression into a magnificent doomfest finale, Bowie-as-narrator reappears with a cathartic address. In a line pilfered from Jacques Brel, his torturous cry of "You're not alone" speaks both to the doomed Ziggy and to his potential audience of star seekers. The payoff, a repeated refrain of "You're wonderful," was a reminder that however much Ziggy was the summation of Bowie's ego ideal, a theatrical sensibility lay at the heart of the work.

"Rock 'n' Roll Suicide" provided the finale to most 1972 shows and all of the shows during 1973 and 1974. It was reactivated for the 1978 world tour. Live versions can be found on *Ziggy Stardust: The Motion Picture, David Live,* and *Stage.*

Although this track-by-track deconstruction of the individual tracks on the album is a necessary part of the album's history, such a detailed breakdown in many ways misses the point. For if *The Rise and Fall of Ziggy Stardust and the Spiders from Mars* is a classic album, it is not by virtue of eleven songs constituting an unimpeachable text. It never quite makes up its mind whether it's a whimsical tale about a fictitious rock 'n' roll band, a detached exercise on the nature of stardom (by someone who'd only tasted it briefly), or simply another collection of David Bowie songs, a handful of which happen to allude to a character called Ziggy.

"Sweet Head," recorded at the November sessions and at least as powerful in its hard rock machinations as anything on the album, was the only recorded song other than "Ziggy Stardust" to specifically name the Ziggy character. It was more avowedly campy and (bi)sexually explicit (the phrase "while yer down there" predates the Bowie/Ronson guitar fellatio routine by several months), making its exclusion from the finished record a mystery. In the light of Bowie's sexually charged image, which exploded prior to the album's release, and the hardening of his band's music over the coming months, it would have been a more appropriate inclusion than, say, "It Ain't Easy." One can only imagine that Bowie wished to keep his options open, playing down the sense of a Ziggy narrative in case the whole idea blew up in his face.

How far Bowie thought he could take the doppelganger idea into his interviews, onto the stage, and perhaps even into his personal life is unclear. The ideas had certainly been fermenting in his mind for the best part of a year by the time the final track selection was made. Bowie had endured years of, if not exactly ridicule, then a general suspicion that he was trying just a little too hard to be taken seriously. When he hooked up with different scenes, be they the Soho Mod clique or the arts lab hairies, his unwillingness to "join the gang" preserved a unique sense of self at the expense of the mistrust of those who had plunged in without reserve.

The Beatles had gotten away with the band-within-a-band idea on *Sgt. Pepper's Lonely Hearts Club Band* because it was just a gimmick on a record heavy with stylistic hooks. By 1972, concept albums were generally conceived along lengthy, mock-classical lines, rather than consisting of eleven three- or four-minute songs. If the Ziggy idea had met with silence or incredulity, then at least the material on the record was sufficiently strong to keep his singer-songwriter guise alive.

The other point worth making about the record at this stage is the aura of electricity that surrounds it, enhanced by the legend "To Be Played at Maximum Volume" on the sleeve (an even stronger demand than Slade's "Play It Loud"). Bowie's acoustic guitar was at least as prominent in the mix as Ronson's, and in 1992, when the album was remastered for reissue on CD, Bowie made it clear that he would have liked the opportunity to have remixed it. A heresy for purists, of course, but evidence that the production was a shade more lightweight than it perhaps should have been. Bearing in mind this was the man who couldn't find a place for "Sweet Head" on the finished master, we have to assume this assessment was made in hindsight.

The sound of an album is—and always has been—just one facet of selling music, whether pop or its more grown-up rock relative. And rarely more so than with *Ziggy Stardust,* a classic album by virtue of its ideological ramifications as much as by what it contained. The importance of the record is to a large extent bound up with a variety of extramusical texts brought into play by Bowie during 1972 and 1973. Stripped of these—the magnification of Bowie as star, the shows that owed as much to theater as to rock 'n' roll, Bowie's collusion with the hype machine, and the issues of identity and gender that were raised along the way, not to mention the phenomenal success of the campaign—*Ziggy Stardust* might just have ended up as a curio, like the Pretty Things' *S.F. Sorrow* or Beggars Opera's *Act One.* As Bowie told William Burroughs late in 1973, "I'm quite certain that the audience that I've got for my stuff don't [*sic*] listen to the lyrics." Although, as his earlier work made clear, he was not averse to writing eight-verse songs, with *Ziggy Stardust,* Bowie came to understand that pop's basic appeal was visual and musical rather than verbal.

One way of helping to "fix" the way a record might be perceived is by its cover (at least in the age of twelve-inch jackets). Compare the surly expressions on the early Rolling Stones album sleeves with the marketing of the cheery Fab Four from Liverpool, and it is easy to see how their public images diverged during the mid-sixties (the reality was rather different). By the early seventies, sleeves bearing the vivid fantasy-driven work of artists such as Roger Dean were a trademark of the progressive genre, an invitation into an otherworld of sound that bore little resemblance to the legend "File Under Popular" often tucked away in a corner of the sleeve.

With the exception of the retracted cartoon sleeve for *The Man Who Sold the World,* Bowie had always gone for a personality shot for his album covers, usually a head-and-shoulders portrait capitalizing on his sensitive good looks. When it came to the sleeve for what turned out to be the greatest costume melodrama in rock, he placed himself in a drab inner-city landscape, a figure not unlike a leprechaun, looking as if he'd just landed from God-knows-where. Gone were the ersatz Hollywood or Rosetti portraits of old: This was Bowie-as-Ziggy, beamed down from the dark sky onto a rainy London side street (outside the K. West furriers at 23 Heddon Street, off Regent Street, to be exact).

Because of Bowie's obsessive attention to the details of his public image, and because the entire Ziggy shebang was defined as much by its visual aspect as its musical texts, it is worth lingering over the album's sleeve. The uncharacteristic projection of the star figure diminished by his surroundings served two purposes. It helped blur the definition between Bowie and Ziggy, a distinction that was further confused by the equal prominence given to "David Bowie" and to "Ziggy Stardust" on the sleeve. It also suggested that for all Bowie/Ziggy's apparent alienness, dressed in his gaily patterned two-piece outfit and purple thigh-high boots, the world in which he found himself was equally foreign, a fact accentuated by the unsettlingly crooked perspective and the unnatural, hand-tinted hue, giving the impression of a noirish Hollywood stage set. There was one puzzling anomaly: If that was Ziggy on the sleeve, then why was he holding his guitar like a right-handed player?

The most prominent single feature on the sleeve is not the star character but the "K. WEST" shop sign above his head. Without suggesting that Bowie was aware of any potential mileage in this at the time, the temptation to speculate on its significance is irresistible. Was not the entire Ziggy escapade the fruition of Bowie's own quest (kwest), an embrace of the Other that lurked within himself? Inhabiting an alter ego that propelled him into the eye of the kind of self-destructive stardom he found so mesmerizing was Bowie's ultimate venture into the unknown.

As an aside, while the struggling younger Bowie was writing songs that despaired of the adult world and revealed a desperate yearning for the purity of childhood, one Keith West was close to topping the U.K. charts with "Excerpt from a Teenage Opera." Better known by its "Grocer Jack" refrain, the single was regarded as an irritant during the Summer of Love, though it shared Bowie's belief that the adult world represented some kind of Fall. But the maudlin chorus of children's voices lamenting the departure of Jack ("Is it true what mummy said, you won't come back?") invested the song with such pathos that even the 1967-era Bowie might have balked at it. The 1972 Bowie would have appreciated its kitsch value.

Flip the *Ziggy Stardust* sleeve over and you find Bowie/Ziggy cocooned from the rest of the world inside a telephone box. The box had an added layer of significance for British audiences: An entire generation had been weaned on the *Dr. Who* television series, where the doctor, a time traveler, hopped from century to century and planet to planet in the Tardis, a high-tech time machine disguised as a telephone box. Unlike the gently macho posturing on the front cover, the Bowie/Ziggy figure inhabiting the box struck a distinctly campy posture, hand on hip and lithe limbed.

THE STAR

At the time the finished master tape was ready (2 February 1972), Bowie's records, led by the just-released *Hunky Dory,* were still selling by the dozen. After its release on 6 June, *The Rise and Fall of Ziggy Stardust and the Spiders from Mars* made a beeline for the U.K. Top 10, and it remained rooted to the charts for the best part of the next eighteen months. (It was a different matter in the States where, despite all the hyperbole, the album actually failed to make the charts.) In complete contrast to the slow-moving "Space Oddity," which took almost three months to achieve its highest U.K. chart place, *Ziggy Stardust* was a shooting star.

A list of hopefuls in the British music press's New Year predictions for 1972 included Linda Lewis, Wishbone Ash, Joe Egan, Dave Lambert, ELO, Lindisfarne, the Natural Acoustic Band, the Strawbs, Annette Peacock, and, as a sop to those who might have wished to tap a foot, the grungy retro rock of those American expatriates the Flamin' Groovies. If any scene was about to go overground, it was expected to be either reggae or jazz rock. The reductionist strain of rock 'n' roll that had been hauled into the public eye with a gloriously vulgar flamboyance by Marc Bolan in the United Kingdom and Alice Cooper in America was hopefully a nasty aberration that would shortly go away. It did not.

Bowie's venture with the Hype at the beginning of 1970 may have been forgotten, but the debate about hyped-up stars selling their souls to the corporate dollar raged on through 1971. That's why Marc Bolan was booed by the apparently discerning crowds at the Weeley Festival of Progressive Music, which took place over a long weekend in August. For

those seeking answers to the failed revolution, looking behind the rhetoric and questioning music industry practices was both sensible and necessary.

The lines of the debate were thrown into confusion by Bowie's arrival during 1972. There is no evidence that the singer ever believed in the power of the alternative rock community to construct a cultural revolution. The superstructure was far too entrenched to succumb to a field full of longhairs spouting ill-digested homilies culled from neo-Marxist texts. Bowie's agenda was firmly rooted in *personal* politics. His instinct told him that the children preferred Coca-Cola to Marx. If he was going to provide them with the pop they wanted, then—to stretch the metaphor to Ziggy-like proportions—it was going to have its own special fizz. That fizz, on which the zeitgeist of the seventies was founded, rejected the outward models of social change for a series of more attainable personal transformations. Out went the old macronarratives of social upheaval; in their place came a series of micronarratives centered on the self: self-discovery, self-love, self-mockery, self-doubt, even self-denial.

In the weeks leading up to Bowie's grand "I'm Gay" gesture in the pages of the rock press in January 1972, there had been features on Leon Russell and Bobby Keyes, session players jettisoned into the public eye by virtue of their unquestionable instrumental talents. Even Elton John, who vied with Marc Bolan for "Pop Star of '71," was complaining about the need for new idols. On 22 January 1972 he got one, served up on the front cover of that week's issue of *Melody Maker*. There he was, cigarette in mouth, wearing his two-piece Ziggy outfit with trouser legs rolled up and the top unzipped to reveal his chest, his newly shorn hair framing his smiling face. The effect was more pancake than beefcake.

The big news stories emblazoned on the cover that week were "[King] Crimson Break Up" and "Big [Jethro] Tull Tour." Bowie's prominent image spoke for itself without such bold type. The small print described him as "rock's swishiest outrage: a self-confessed lover of effeminate clothes, Bowie, who has hardly performed in public since his 'Space Oddity' hit of three years ago, is coming back in super-style." The piece, which couldn't have been written any more effusively had it been penned by Defries himself, claimed that the American press was already calling Bowie the new Dylan, that *Hunky Dory* was about to make the charts in the United Kingdom, and that the single lifted from that album, "Changes," had recently made "Record of the Week" on Tony Blackburn's Radio 1 show. "Breathless for more? Turn to page 19."

And there it was, three paragraphs into Michael Watts's "Oh You Pretty Thing" piece. "He's gay, he says. Mmmmmmm." Further down the column, Watts reminds us: "He supposes he's what people call bisexual." And what about that dress? "Oh dear, you must understand that it's not a woman's. It's a man's dress."

Having snapped at the bait, readers were invited to sample the rest of the Bowie manifesto. How he enjoyed "flower power" but was far keener to preserve his individuality; that "he says he's more an actor and entertainer than a musician"; how "everyone just knows that David is going to be a lollapalooza of a superstar throughout the entire world this year," not least the star-in-waiting himself, with a revealing "I'm going to be huge, and it's quite frightening in a way." And, no doubt drawing on his own experience, Bowie offered an explanation for the contemporary disintegration of identity: "I think that we have created a new kind of person in a way. We have created a child who will be so exposed to the media that he will be lost to his parents by the time he is twelve."

When Bowie had played one of his rare 1971 shows in Aylesbury in September, he had had long hair and had been billed as "The Man Who Sold the World." On 29 January, a week after the infamous *Melody Maker* report, he returned as "The Most Beautiful Person in the World." The advertisement made no mention of Ziggy or the Spiders, although the image had been drastically altered: This was simply "David Bowie with his musicians." Incongruously, there was a vaguely hippieish message tucked away below: "Homo Superiors . . . Bells . . . Feet . . . Worlds . . . Hello."

The two national tours that followed, from February to March and from April to mid-July, didn't exactly bear out Bowie's claim to imminent megastar status. In fact, many of these theater-sized venues were half empty, although enthusiasm among those who did show up was almost conspiratorial. But if the self-styled "star" tag was going to take a little while to sink in, the gender tourism (Bowie was married and a father) stuck. "Best thing I ever said, I suppose," he recalled in 1976. When the singer "went down" on Mick Ronson during "Suffragette City" at a gig in Oxford on 17 June, Bowie's in-house photographer Mick Rock was there to capture the seminal image, which was quickly distributed by RCA. Weeks later, *Gay News* reporter Peter Holmes enthused: "David Bowie is probably the best rock musician in Britain now. One day, he'll become as popular as he deserves to be. And that'll give gay rock a potent spokesman."

It wasn't that simple. Had a sizable percentage of his audience really believed he was gay, would they still have bought his records? Why, for example, did Elton John see fit to conceal his homosexuality for another decade? Ditto Freddie Mercury? And what about those other stars who still cannot admit their true sexual preferences? And why was Angie Bowie plastered all over the press during 1973, as Bowie made the transition from cult phenomenon to international superstar?

The answers came thick and fast. The lead letter to *Melody Maker* in the wake of the January cover story suggested a new "fag rock" genre, and wondered whether we might yet see Elvis in drag. Tabloid muckraker Jean Rook pandered to her *Daily Express* readership with an uncharacteristically subtle gibe at "the pop star with the poison green eyelids and the hair like an orange lavatory brush." And when the Bowie circus arrived in the States, it prompted Robert Christgau to speculate whether "songs about Andy Warhol written by an English fairy are enough for American audiences." Meanwhile, rock journalist Lester Bangs vented his stream-of-consciousness spleen in *Creem* with a surfeit of "Faggot Rock" references.

Bowie's "gayness" worked on several levels. First and foremost it was seen as a piece of rock theater, another in a long line of "mock-shock" headlines that even homophobes could talk themselves into finding excusable. Why, it could even have been Ziggy speaking. It certainly didn't stop girls (and women) trying to get into his pants, and if legend is to be believed, quite a lot of them did. In this endeavor, it may even have worked to his advantage, providing added bait to those who suspected Bowie was as tight-arsed as those opportunists who swapped their denims for glad rags after so-called camp rock became fashionable.

Frankly, the truth of Bowie's sexual inclination was (and is) of little importance. The point was that his dramatic intervention, at a time when gender was becoming increasingly politicized, gave a window to a generation of teenagers cast adrift from the sexual certainties of their peers. For Bowie, the expression of sexual freedom might merely have made manifest one part of his intellectual quest to embrace Otherness. Recalling in the eighties that Bowie had offered him an olive branch of hope, Boy George spoke for thousands of others coming to terms with the nature of their sexuality in the early seventies. As Jon Savage has noted, Bowie made homosexuality attractive, liberating it from the pantomime dame routine and the limp-wristed comic stereotype and investing it with rock-star chic. Within months, every band—at least in Britain—had one token "gay" member who'd camp it up for the *Top of the Pops* cameras.

A bastardization, for sure, but for such a dispersal of accepted "maleness" to occur, and so quickly, marked some kind of breakthrough. (The well-documented chant of "pooftahs" that greeted Roxy Music—fellow travelers who also drew on a palette culled from a variety of past rock and pop styles—at the Liverpool Stadium that year suggested it was going to be a long haul.) Nevertheless, in the wake of *Ziggy*, "gay" was beginning to be associated with fun, not furtive encounters.

As much as the "I'm Gay" tag had sensationalized Bowie, making him the most talked-about would-be star of 1972, the rhetoric was nevertheless subsumed by the projection of otherworldly and futuristic alienness. The taboo of homosexuality was thus tempered by the irresistible allure of the extraordinary, a continuation of the flouting of convention that had delivered David Jones to the world of pop during the late fifties and had drawn many identity seekers after him. By declaring himself as—and having transformed his body into—a spectacle of indeterminate sexuality, he was in many ways a logical extension of past crises prompted by Elvis, Mick Jagger, and the "unisex" hippies.

By mid-1972, Bowie's backing band of Ronson, Bolder, and Woodmansey had also begun to adopt glitzy costumes, serving to emphasize a sense of theater over any more daring subtext. Bowie's emaciated, hairless body with the pallor of a corpse remained the central focus, but with the Spiders from Mars (which was how Bowie had begun to introduce his band onstage in March of 1972) now sparkling strangely behind him, the invitation was not merely to join the "starman" Bowie on his peculiar quest, but to become part of his vogueish "gang." This owed much to the lingering taste left by *A Clockwork Orange,* a film that, according to its publicity, concerned "the adventures of a young man whose principal interests are rape, ultra-violence and Beethoven."

Bowie now acknowledges his debt to the sartorial strangeness of Malcolm McDowell and his deviant band of Droogies. "I got most of the look for Ziggy [from] that," he said in 1993. "The jumpsuits I thought were just wonderful, and I liked the malicious, malevolent, vicious quality of those four guys, although aspects of violence themselves didn't turn me on particularly. I wanted to put another spin on that, so . . . I picked out all these florid, bright, quilted kind of materials. That took the edge off the violent look of those suits, but still retained that terrorist, we're-ready-for-action kind of [image]." The projection of the "lightning flash" symbol as a backdrop on later Ziggy tours emphasized this element, as well as, more worryingly, connotations with the Nazi SS.

The associations with *A Clockwork Orange* helped give Ziggy a sense of danger that, along with the space invader–like aspect of his image, widened the visual appeal. But these capricious shifts in style, which became ever more marked as the Ziggy show was taken to America and then on to Japan, were underpinned by an artfulness that served to emphasize the unnaturalness of stardom. Riding on the back of an album that blurred the relationship between artist and character, Bowie became, in many ways, the first postmodern rock star.

Susan Sontag, in her influential essay "Notes on Camp," suggests that the essence of camp is its love of the unnatural, of artifice, of exaggeration: "Camp sees everything in quotation-marks. . . . To perceive Camp in objects and persons is to understand Being-as-Playing-a-Role. It is the fullest extension, in sensibility, of the metaphor of life as theater." And what had Sontag identified as "one of the great images of Camp"? The androgyne.

Had they not been penned in 1964, her words could have been written with Bowie in mind—though Bowie never lost sight of the business of securing his own success, by creating a persona on record, and then stepping more fully into that character for his public appearances. Had the entire project ended in failure, Bowie's ego would probably still have remained intact, protected by the armor of those all-important quotation marks (unless, perhaps, the psychic scars left by Terry had cut deeper than he had supposed).

This camp sensibility also sheds light on Bowie's comments to John Mendelsohn back in 1971, when he depicted the relationship between music and performer as being akin to that between mask and message. According to Sontag, "The whole point of Camp is to dethrone the serious. . . . Camp involves a new, more complex relation to 'the serious.' One can be serious about the frivolous, frivolous about the serious." Bowie's plaything was rock itself. His uncertain attitude toward it mirrored the inner conflicts that continued to pull at his own sense of identity. As he told Charles Shaar Murray in 1974, "The rock business has become so established, and so much like a society, that I have revolted against it. That's what wasn't liked; that I won't take it seriously, and I'll break its rules. . . . That's why I felt naturally inclined to take the piss out of it."

Tony Defries's promotion machine hit warp factor ten during the early months of 1972, preparing the ground for Ziggy's arrival. In May, after twenty shows earlier in the year, the well-rehearsed band was unveiled to a batch of journalists invited to a performance at Kingston Polytechnic. *Disc* magazine couldn't let this pass without comment: "David Bowie must be coming up for the 'Most Reviewed Act In The

Shortest Time' award," wrote their cynical, if otherwise enthusiastic, eye-witness.

In addition to magazine features (few interviews with Bowie were granted immediately before the album's release, thus creating an aura of exclusivity around him) and live reviews, there was the added weight of RCA's advertising campaign, which began in January with the relatively low key promotion of *Hunky Dory* but went into overload from June onward. The album, the singles "John, I'm Only Dancing" and "The Jean Genie," the tours and prestigious one-off shows, the reissuing of his 1969 album (retitled *Space Oddity*) and *The Man Who Sold the World* (both given Ziggy-like covers), even personal messages to his fans and supporters—"Thanx to all 'OUR' people for making ZIGGY. I love you. Bowie x"—were trumpeted with full-page ads. It didn't stop there: At the end of the shows, fans were often showered with photos and posters.

To prepare the way for Ziggy's arrival in America, shortly after the release of the album, in July 1972, Defries flew a posse of that country's most influential journalists (representing *Rolling Stone,* the *New York Times, Interview, Creem,* and the *New Yorker*) to England for a showcase performance, again in the Bowie-friendly environment of Aylesbury, Bucks. The following day, the transatlantic throng were assembled, along with British counterparts, for a press conference at the Dorchester Hotel, one of London's top hostelries. Photographers were banned. Instructions were issued that David was not to be touched. And on the top table, flanking David and Angie, were the two godfathers of American subterranean rock, Lou Reed and Iggy Pop. Both had just made their respective London debuts at the King's Cross Cinema.

The pair were there to lend weight to the theory that Bowie was not simply a media construction, a star so plastic you could almost see him melting. Reed and Iggy Pop were the living embodiment of a tradition that Bowie had now joined himself: the Warholian superstar that Lou Reed should have been, the deviant showman that Iggy was (though few outside of Detroit and New York had ever seen the real thing). Here was the man whose praises Bowie had often sung during his gigs before launching into "White Light/White Heat" and "Waiting for the Man" and who had recently joined Bowie onstage at the Festival Hall for messy revivals of three Velvet Underground songs. As for Iggy Pop, was he not the "leper messiah" in person?

ENTS COMMITTEE
POLYTECHNIC
of CENTRAL LONDON
115 NEW CAVENDISH STREET W1 tel 01-580 8799

Friday, May 12th   Doors open 7 30

Only Central London appearance of

DAVID BOWIE

with GOOD HABIT

Admission 60p Adv tickets from Students' Union

Tickets on sale at Virgin Records

⊖ Gt. Portland St.   ⊖ Warren Str

The two Americans, with whom Bowie was now said to be working (on Reed's *Transformer* and Iggy Pop's *Raw Power*), were there to confirm Bowie's auteur status. He was making himself the titular head of a hitherto ignored tradition, one that rejected the lofty ideals of musical advancement in favor of a trash aesthetic with artsy overtones. Never mind that Stooges bassist Ron Asheton later complained of "Bowie and Iggy's cocaine artsy-fartsy mix . . . Bowie . . . just fucked that album up! Really fucked it." Or that *Transformer* was, in the esteemed view of *New Musical Express* writer Nick Kent, "a total parody of Reed's whole style." The point, as far as Bowie and his fans were concerned, was that he was becoming the one-man revolution of his wildest fantasies.

He'd even written his own anthem around which this new strain of outré glamour could congregate. Titling it "All the Young Dudes," he had presented it to Mott the Hoople, a ballsy rock 'n' roll band whose inability to translate the excitement of their live shows onto record had prompted them to split up earlier that spring after recording three albums for Island. Bowie tempted them back into the studio, produced and arranged the sessions for the *Dudes* album, and took the plaudits when the single gave the band a huge hit, revitalizing their career in the process. Tony Defries tied up the business side of things, securing a £50,000 deal with CBS. The relationship quickly soured: Mott the Hoople became the first band (but certainly not the last) to flee the manager's newly constituted Mainman stable. Conveniently, "All the Young Dudes" drew on aspects of the Ziggy mythology, with its references to suicide, dressing "like a Queen," "ripping off the stars from his face," and "kicking it in the head when he was twenty-five."

As for the record on which Bowie's part-plastic star was hung, *The Rise and Fall of Ziggy Stardust and the Spiders from Mars,* it had become an instant success, chained to the U.K. charts for the rest of the year and beyond. Claims by the end of 1972 that the album had sold a million copies were typical Mainman hyperbole: It had sold just short of 100,000 copies in the United Kingdom, and a similar figure in the States. It was not even the biggest album of the year, although the end-of-year critics polls tended to suggest it was the most important. *Melody Maker,* the magazine that had started the ball rolling back in January, had made the most of its foresight, putting Bowie back on its cover. And, of course, the magazine gave itself a big pat on the back: "The Man Who Sold the World . . . Well, not yet, but David Bowie was certainly THE main man of 1972, just as we predicted when we front-paged him back in January." (But whatever happened to Dave Lambert, the Natural Acoustic Band, and Annette Peacock . . . ?)

The otherworld of stardom, which had seduced Bowie ever since he had set his prepubescent eyes on those big-screen Hollywood creations, was now his. But the rise was only one part of the bargain. For Bowie, stardom was not merely an escape from anonymity, his way of leaving his fingerprint on history. It was a flight from the suspicion that he had no fingerprint to leave. To apply poststructuralist terms, the intrusion of Ziggy signified the death of the subject. As Bowie said in 1976, "Being famous helps put off the problems of discovering myself. I mean that."

But maybe stardom merely exacerbated the problem, something critic David Hatch picked up on when he characterized Ziggy's rise and fall as a vicious circle where "the greater the acclaim, the wider the separation, both physical and intellectual, between performer and listener, resulting in the ultimate destruction of the star by his followers and the collapse of the myth." While reading Oscar Wilde's *Picture Of Dorian Gray* during his days with Ken Pitt, Bowie would have no doubt stumbled upon the following aphorism: "It is the spectator, and not life, that art really mirrors." There was no more diligent spectator of David Bowie than Bowie himself, and his art, in the form of Ziggy's rise and fall, now presented him with a reflection he couldn't resist.

ODEON THEATRE
ROMFORD

MEL BUSH presents
DAVID BOWIE

TUESDAY
MAY **22**
at 8-0 p.m.
DOORS OPEN 7-15 p.m.

STALLS
£1·80 **H21**
INCL. VAT

SMOKING NOT PERMITTED
No ticket exchanged nor money refunded
THIS PORTION TO BE RETAINED

THE MASQUERADE

I FELT LIKE AN ACTOR.

—"Five Years," from *The Rise*
and Fall of Ziggy Stardust and the Spiders from Mars

CAN'T TELL 'EM APART AT ALL.

—"Andy Warhol," from
***Hunky Dory*, 1971**

As the Ziggy concerts drew bigger crowds, forcing the show into larger venues, the stage presentation became ever more dramatic, fulfilling the "pantomime rock" style identified by journalist John Mendelsohn back in 1971. Prior to the first Ziggy concerts in January 1972, Bowie told George Tremlett that his new act would be "theatrical," and "[a kind of] entertainment . . . quite different to anything anyone else has tried to do before . . . there's not much outrageousness left in pop music anymore—there's only me and Marc Bolan."

He carefully avoided mention of Alice Cooper, whose London debut at the Rainbow Theatre in November 1971 had been as shocking a visual spectacle as anything seen on a British stage up to that point. That performance had been based on Cooper's *Killer* album, where Alice had acted out the part of a nasty boy, with the aid of a real live boa constrictor, a hammer, and a sword. But it was nothing more than an old-fashioned morality play: Alice was forced into a straitjacket and "executed" in

David Bowie
MICK ROCK, COURTESY OF
STAR FILE

103

an electric chair for his sins. "The bad guy always got his punishment," wrote guitarist Michael Bruce in his recent memoirs.

Beneath the glitzy Hammer Horror, Alice was one of the guys, enjoying nothing better than a few cans of Bud and settling down to his favorite television soap opera after a hard day's night onstage. The chasm between the public and the private Alice was about as wide as the trouser legs Bowie had sported on the back of the *Hunky Dory* sleeve. It was pure sensationalism, appealing to a sense of outrage that pitted kids against their parents, but no more threatening than an American fifties B movie where good always triumphed over the alien menace in the end.

It is just possible that Bowie's well-documented dismissal of Cooper wasn't purely based on ideological differences. In the mid-sixties, Alice—as plain old Vincent Furnier from Michigan—had fronted an R&B cover band called the Spiders, who then briefly became the Nazz. As Alice Cooper, he enjoyed a gay following who lapped up what many considered to be the worst band in the world with all the ironic sensibility they could muster. Like Bowie, the Alice Cooper band had seen the potential of the new teenage audience, even going so far as to write an anthem, "I'm Eighteen," for the market that rock was in danger of forgetting. And by the summer of 1972, Alice Cooper had even one-upped Bowie's "All the Young Dudes" with "School's Out," the perfect way to celebrate the arrival of the summer vacation.

While Cooper had set the tone for a new vaudeville, the multifaceted Bowie—an acknowledged songwriter and a pop theorist—translated it into an art form. He was Citizen Arcane to Cooper's Depression-beating Gold Digger of 1972. Both played the showman with consummate opportunism, enhancing their careers immeasurably by giving back to audiences the spectacle they'd been missing, but Bowie's carnivalesque creation was different on two crucial levels.

RAINBOW PAVILION

Torbay's new Rock venue
on the Harbour Site

Sunday, 2nd July

DAVID BOWIE

Tickets from Box Office

Sunday, 9th July

LINDISFARNE

Both Cooper and Bowie had acted out roles with the detachment of a neutral observer and an irony that rejoiced in puncturing the prevailing rock ideology. The difference was that Bowie had not killed off the romantic image of the truth-seeking rock Renaissance man. He'd simply altered the rules to suit his own obsession with the feeling of emptiness at the heart of his own identity. By 1972, all the soul searching of the late sixties had amounted to nothing. The suggestion that self-emancipation could be arrived at by denial of self rather than some humanistically charged belief in self-enlightenment was no less an idealization than, say, Lennon baring his soul on the 1970 album *Plastic Ono Band.* Holes, not "whole." Simon Frith understood the irony of the situation when he wrote: "What they [Bowie and Bryan Ferry] did was redefine progressive rock, revitalising the idea of the Romantic artist in terms of media fame."

Bowie implicitly understood himself to be a social construct, a reflection of whatever he was exposed to, or—and here's where the notion of human agency comes in—chose to expose himself to. "I'm really just a photostat machine," he said in July 1973. "I pour out what

FRIARS MARKET SQUARE **AYLESBURY**

Saturday, January 29th, 7 30
THE MOST BEAUTIFUL PERSON IN THE WORLD

DAVID BOWIE

WITH HIS MUSICIANS

AND ALSO **GRAND CANYON**
ALPHA CENTAURI LIGHTS · CANYON SOUNDS
Tickets 60p from Earth Records, Aylesbury, or 65p at the door
Membership 15p
A rare chance to see one of the world's finest live performers in
Britain's nicest club
HOMO SUPERIORS .. BELLS .. FEET ... WORLDS . HELLO

has already been fed in. I merely reflect what is going on around me." Dave Laing, in *One Chord Wonders,* recognized Bowie's auteurist tendencies when he summarized the Ziggy episode thus: "The intention, on record and live performance, was strictly dramatic. Though dressed as Ziggy Stardust and singing his songs as well as those of the album's narrator, Bowie intended to signify Ziggy, not become him." But denying the slippage between Bowie and Ziggy ignores the long-festering forces that climaxed in Ziggy's creation, and the full meaning of Bowie's I'll-be-your-mirror method of dealing with his own struggle for identity.

Thus Bowie's slide into character was as wish-fulfilling as it was essential to his artistic credo. As one rifles through the sheaves of interviews and press cuttings relating to the Ziggy era, it is this idea of the star as the source of ultimate satisfaction that emerges time and again. Just as the boundaries between Bowie and Ziggy became increasingly blurred as Bowie's fame rose to Promethean proportions, so were the boundaries between music and the practices that revolved around it. Relatively little was written about the music Bowie was making during 1972 and 1973. His success opened a can of worms for critics, whose previous view of what was "false" (pop) and what was "real" (rock) in popular music was thrown into confusion by this novel, genre-straddling perspective.

So, too, was Bowie. The Ziggy spectacle had been transformed from a flashy rock 'n' roll show during the spring and early summer tours into full-blown rock theater at the Rainbow in August. During this six months of regular touring, seven songs from *Ziggy Stardust* formed a regular part of the set, with "Soul Love," "Lady Stardust," "It Ain't Easy," and "Star" largely absent (in fact, the latter two songs were never publicly aired during the Ziggy era).

At least as many songs performed during the two U.K. spring tours were drawn from Bowie's most recent album, *Hunky Dory:* "The Superman," "Queen Bitch," "Song for Bob Dylan," "Andy Warhol," "Changes," and "Life on Mars." Apart from "Queen Bitch," these songs clearly rooted Bowie in the Anglo-American songwriter genre. The presence of "Space Oddity" was an obvious reminder of his chart pedigree, and at the same time it reinforced the idea that the *Ziggy Stardust* material was perhaps part of an enduring cosmic obsession. A cover of Jacques

Brel's "Port of Amsterdam" brought a hint of Eurodecadence to the show, though Bowie later replaced it with "My Death." This song was more obviously appropriate for the Ziggy plot, serving as a premonition for the character's eventual demise. Another cover, Chuck Berry's "Round and Round," recorded for *Ziggy Stardust* but dropped from the final track list, helped bind Bowie to the vogueish tendency to reinvoke rock's early primitivism, asserting that he was, in the final analysis, simply a rock 'n' roller.

Despite Bowie's satin costumes and knee-high boxing boots, and Ronno's increasing confidence in stepping out in sequined jackets, red lipstick, and peroxided hair, the element of theatricality so crucial to the entire Ziggy project was, at this stage, only marginally more sartorially flashy than that of any other act who chose to shop at the fashionable Alkasura boutique. The shows were tight and conformed to the age-old formula: Get 'em going, calm 'em down, and pull out all stops for the finale.

A central difference between the lure of the Ziggy project and that of other acts was the starry aura that Bowie was increasingly able to carry off as audiences grew and his confidence rose. By the time of the Royal Festival Hall show on 8 July, this had become apparent to Ray Coleman, who wrote in *Melody Maker,* "Bowie is a flashback in many ways to the pop star theatres of about ten years ago, carrying on a detached love affair with his audience, wooing them, yet never surrendering that vital aloofness that makes him untouchable."

Theater, detachment: Those two words, which had become virtually off limits in the aesthetics of contemporary rock, were for Bowie intrinsic to the projection of himself and to his perception of the pop-music archetype. Once *Ziggy Stardust* had been released and its conceptual matter digested, he seized the moment to transform his glammed-up rock 'n' roll show (laced with a twist of kudos-earning songwriting artistry) into a full-fledged theatrical performance. Understood in the context of the self-reflective *Ziggy Stardust* album, it was always likely to be received as something more than a Screaming Lord Sutch–like publicity stunt. The Ziggy concerts became an integral part of a new critical commentary on the very nature of performance and stardom.

The new show was unveiled at the Rainbow Theatre on 19 August 1972. The performance area was elaborately designed, incorporating split-level movable scaffolding. Images were projected on to a backdrop, the Astronettes (his back-up singers) danced wildly, and dry ice transformed the stage into a virtual Hammer Horror set. Charles Shaar Murray was in no doubt about the epochal nature of the performance, writing in the *New Musical Express,* "A Bowie concert is your old Busby Berkeley production . . . this was perhaps the most consciously theatrical rock show ever staged." For added dramatic tension, the band walked onto the stage to the sounds of Beethoven's "Ode To Joy," which, owing to its use in *A Clockwork Orange,* invoked an aura of imminent social breakdown. The bigger-is-better philosophy was also applied to the music: Piano and sax were added to flesh out the sound.

According to the Gillmans, at the start of September, shortly before liftoff for the first U.S. tour, Tony Defries energized Bowie's growing entourage with one of his customary pep talks. "So far as RCA in America is concerned," he said, "the man with the red hair at the end of the table is the biggest thing to have come out of England since the Beatles—and possibly before the Beatles. . . . You've all got to learn how to look and act like a million dollars."

With Britain eating out of Bowie's generously extended hands, Defries had recently decided to relocate his Mainman management offices to New York. He'd also recruited several ex–cast members from *Pork,* including Tony Zanetta, Leee Black Childers, and Cherry Vanilla, to assist in the operation. It was a gamble, for none had any real experience in record company promotion, but what better way to advertise the unfathomable strangeness of his star than by unleashing this bizarre group of fast-talking, loud-dressing motormouths on the American press. Even if the scribes were left unconvinced by Bowie's performances, they'd at least be able to write about his cronies, who included a fleet of burly bodyguards with orders to protect their fragile charge by whatever means necessary.

Selling Bowie to Britain had largely been a matter of winning over the London-based journalists. In America, which was made up of more states than Bowie had selves, the Mainman machine couldn't hope to reach all areas. In Kansas City, for example, only 250 people turned up for the show, recalling Bowie's grin-and-bear-it days playing the club circuit. In St. Louis, it was even worse: Ziggy played to just 110 paying customers. But on the East and West coasts (not forgetting Detroit and

Cleveland, strongholds of a subterranean rock tradition), Bowie at least received prominent reviews. Some critics, including Robert Christgau in the *New Yorker,* complained that he was "currently trying to ride a massive hype into superstardom"; others, such as Lillian Roxon in the *New York Daily News,* reveled in "Star Is Born" hyperbole.

For the American visit, which ran through December, the set developed into something approaching a full-fledged Ziggy show. Out went the familiar covers like Chuck Berry's "Round and Round," Cream's "I Feel Free," and the Who's "I Can't Explain." There was no place, either, for two more gentle numbers from Bowie's own catalog, "Wild Eyed Boy from Freecloud" and "Song for Bob Dylan." In their place came three new songs, "John, I'm Only Dancing" (recorded at Trident during the summer), and "The Jean Genie" and "Drive-In Saturday," written while traveling across the country. In contrast to the *Ziggy Stardust* material, there was little indication that this new material was written with anything like the same kind of knowing detachment. The strong narrative streak that had informed songs like "Starman" and "Ziggy Stardust" had given way to a more thorough immersion into rock-star decadence: Bowie was now writing from within his all-conquering character.

"John, I'm Only Dancing," which became Bowie's last U.K. single of 1972, was a mildly sophisticated exercise in Velvet Undergound–inspired minimalism, its tight, intense rhythm bringing to mind the fantasy that if German experimental band Can had made a stab at the pop market, the result might have sounded something like this. Lyrically, it flirted freely with overblown campy sensibility, a point emphasized by its shrill, histrionic delivery. The single was considered too outré for the American market.

Bowie, with his vast entourage of what most observers took to be the most cliquey rock 'n' roll circus ever to waltz through the country, wrote continually while on the road in America. The results were heard on *Aladdin Sane,* issued in April 1973, an album that was everything *Ziggy Stardust* could only aspire to be. As Bowie told BBC Radio's Stuart Grundy in 1976, "*Aladdin Sane* was *Ziggy Stardust* meets 'Fame.' *Ziggy Stardust* the album was an objective point-of-view album, and *Aladdin Sane* was himself talking about being a star and hitting America. I'd had that first experience of America, so I had plenty of material for it. So it was a subjective Ziggy talking, really."

Much cruder in its execution than *Ziggy Stardust, Aladdin Sane* eschewed the plot/conceptual format of its predecessor. That artistic device was no longer necessary: The wish fulfilled, Bowie was now writing from the point of view of his magnified creation. As he had always suspected, and probably hoped, the apparent reality of that situation was clouded by a different kind of detachment.

Cut off from the mundane details of day-to-day living, pampered by a retinue of gofers and well-wishers, swapping the domesticity of Beckenham for a fleeting series of interiors (hotels, rented limousines, and concert theaters), and increasingly reliant on a diet of confidence-sustaining drugs, he was caught in a dizzying "crash-course for the ravers," an actor all too aware of the cracks in his mask; hence, "A Lad Insane." What more appropriate symbol for this ultimate destination than the red-and-blue "flash," an international sign for danger, that covered the right side of his face on the cover photograph.

Though his American sojourn had delivered little in terms of chart success and had resulted in deficits on both RCA's and Mainman's balance sheets, Bowie returned to the United Kingdom in December as if he'd tamed the biggest market in the world. The show, which had grown increasingly theatrical, was by now an unquestionably rock 'n' roll–heavy set that had largely dispensed with the quieter pieces from his pre–*Ziggy Stardust* work, and his two biggest hits, "Space Oddity" and "Starman." Several numbers shorter than his summer of 1972 shows, the only notable addition to the set was the inclusion of "Let's Spend the Night Together," an audacious revival of the Rolling Stones' controversial 1967 hit, which was given an added layer of meaning in the face of Bowie's ambisexual persona. As the opening number, it established a more flamboyant tone that was interrupted only by the "Changes"/"The Superman"/"Life on Mars?" trilogy and the lengthy "The Width of a Circle," a cue for a mime sequence based on a crude "flight to freedom" metaphor.

In February of 1973, after just two months back in the United Kingdom, where he played a handful of shows, Bowie returned to America with a more carefully constructed tour itinerary and a depleted entourage. Onstage, though, his band had doubled in size with the addition of horn players Ken Fordham and Brian Wilshaw, modern jazz pianist Mike Garson, and old pals Hutch and Geoff McCormack on guitar and backing vocals, respectively. The assumption was that America—a land intensely proud of its own scale—preferred its music larger, louder, and more technically proficient.

For this second visit, Bowie drastically altered his set in order to preview more of the *Aladdin Sane* material, although in a typical show six *Ziggy Stardust* songs remained, with "Rock 'n' roll Suicide" the inevitable show-closer. At a concert held at Radio City Music Hall in New York in mid-February—by which time Bowie was making up to a half-dozen costume changes per night—he was halfway through "Rock 'n' Roll Suicide" when a fan jumped onstage and kissed his cheek. Bowie collapsed in a heap and was promptly carried offstage. An audience recording captures the flavor of the moment when Ziggy was (briefly) seen to die on stage: "Oh, I don't believe it . . . Oh my God, oh . . . What happened?" "He's alright, he collapsed." "Why did that kid do that?" Some swear they heard gunshots ring out in the concert hall.

If the audience was beginning to conflate Ziggy's fictional demise with the reality of a David Bowie performance, there was little doubt that the man himself was also succumbing to the self-effacing charms of the imaginary. For the past twelve months, he'd been introducing his band as the Spiders, and while stopping short of referring to himself as Ziggy, stepping into the shoes of his archetypal rock 'n' roll creation was as easy as it was necessary in order to build on his own myth. Liberated from the watchful eye of self-consciousness, it was much simpler to "play it too far" from behind a smoke screen.

Mick Ronson hinted at this shortly before his death when he told Tony Parsons, "Ziggy definitely affected him. To do anything and to do it well, you have to become completely involved. He had to become what Ziggy was; he had to believe in him. Yes, Ziggy affected his personality. But he affected Ziggy's personality. They lived off each other." But Bowie the ever-changing man knew that there could be only one survivor in this battle of ego and alter ego. Having already suffered typecasting with "Space Oddity," and acutely aware that star personae could quickly become tired and ineffectual, the Bowie camp began circulating noises of imminent change. The sense of imminent "death" was already beginning to infiltrate the music press back home, with *Melody Maker* splashing the question "Bowie's Last Tour?" on its front page in February.

Meanwhile, there was the rest of the world tour to think about. That fatigue was setting in was reflected in the abbreviated set list for the Japanese leg of the tour. Two songs, "Starman" and "Round and Round," were reinstated, at the expense of "Soul Love," "My Death," "Drive-In Saturday," "Aladdin Sane," "Panic in Detroit," "Cracked Actor," "The Prettiest Star," and "Suffragette City."

That spring, Bowie returned to the United Kingdom to find that the country had gone, in the words of *Melody Maker,* "Bowie mad!" His early summer tour had sold out in a matter of days; "Drive-In Saturday" reached the Top 3, followed by a belated release of the single "Life on Mars?"; and five Bowie titles figured on the album chart. Far from being a temporary blip—or, to some, blot—on the pop landscape, glam rock had assumed epidemic proportions. The plethora of one-time bubblegum hits, with occasional murmurings from hard-rock acts that had reigned between 1970 and 1972, had been supplanted by an invasion of silver-foil rockers: Slade, Sweet, Wizzard, Geordie, Suzi Quatro, and the crudest glam rocker of all, the reinvigorated old rock 'n' roller Gary Glitter, had all seized the moment. Suddenly, it was Christmas all year 'round. The glam rock that had been introduced with panache by Marc Bolan and given an air of sophistication by David Bowie had been reduced to a litany of anthems delivered by a seemingly endless parade of opportunistic wave catchers.

Few, if any, of these acts managed to unite the pop and rock markets in the way Bowie did. No great personality cults had grown up around Slade's Noddy Holder or Sweet's Brian Connolly. Devoid of edge and lacking unfathomable mystery, they were mere Cliff Richardses to his Vince Taylor, although Bowie, despite his entry into an ever-spiraling whirlwind of hokey-cokey stardom, could never emulate Taylor's genuine abandon.

That didn't stop him from trying. The final Ziggy tour, a mad, celebratory jaunt around Britain from May to July, ended in a manner akin to Taylor's own self-immolation in Paris several years earlier. This time, there were no white robes or declamatory speeches pertaining to the star's Christ-like róle. But for the audience at the Hammersmith Odeon on 3 July, the final night of the tour, it was as if a savior had relinquished his role. Toward the end of the show, Bowie stepped up to the mike to thank everyone for "one of the greatest tours of our lives." His final words have since gone down as some of the most infamous in rock 'n' roll mythology:

"Not only is it the last show of the tour, but it's the last show that we'll ever do. Thank you."

Bowie had effectively cemented the bond between himself and his creation, and in a way that entirely befitted the theatrical sensibility that fueled his transformation from also-ran to what Defries was already calling "Man of the Decade." As if witnessing a real death, the audience gasped. Woody Woodmansey (who, unlike Mick Ronson and Bowie's aides-de-camp, was not prepared for this), reportedly threw his drumstick in Bowie's direction—he was out of a job. Ziggy's metaphorical fall had been made complete. He was killed off four years to the day after the death of Rolling Stone Brian Jones, and two years after the Doors' Jim Morrison was found dead in his bath in Paris. Ziggy, too, was about to enter rock's hallowed crypt.

Despite the suggestion that Bowie had had it with rock 'n' roll, that he was about to move into films, playing the role of Michael Valentine Smith in a big-screen version of Robert Heinlein's *Stranger in a Strange Land,* he was back in the studio within a matter of weeks. The resulting album, *Pin Ups,* was yet another exercise in self-mythology: Now that Bowie's own life and career were wholly entwined with his Ziggy creation, this nostalgic celebration of the music of Swinging London can be seen as Ziggy's last fling, another pastiche of pop's past dressed up by locating the character's prehistory in less complicated times. Why else would Bowie have chosen to close the album with a version of the Kinks' rhetorical "Where Have All the Good Times Gone?"

The good times were certainly fast disappearing from Bowie's own life, as he'd suggested to Roy Hollingworth from *Melody Maker* in May. "I'm sick of being Gulliver," he said. "You know, after America, Moscow, Siberia, Japan. I just want to bloody well go home to Beckenham and watch the telly." Drained by the events of the past eighteen months, which had started out with a knowing commentary on stardom and ended in virtual physical and mental collapse, Bowie had eased himself out of the role with a stopgap album of covers and some half-formed fantasies of making Ziggy into a full-length television spectacular. One of these efforts helped maintain his public profile; the other came to nothing, though a discussion of a Ziggy stage production with writer William Burroughs made entertaining copy when published in the February 1974 edition of *Rolling Stone.*

Titled "Beat Writer Meets Glitter Mainman," the piece revealed Bowie as a reflection of his new mentor. The show would be a forty-act performance, he said, cut up so that the scenes would be played at random. Ziggy would now be recast in the manner of a Burroughsian sci-fi epic, overflowing with dystopian and conspiracy-theory overtones. Ziggy would no longer be a screen for Bowie or his audiences to project their fantasies onto, but a vehicle for what he called "the Infinites." Spent with being David Bowie or Ziggy Stardust, his quest for self-effacement had now taken him beyond Warholian whiteout: The Infinites were not people but black holes. The author had finally declared himself absent. It would be a long, slow haul back.

Postscript

Ten, nine, eight . . .

The countdown to the point of no return, where characters on a computer disk finally set off to become words in a book, has begun. On the other side of the Atlantic, and having no cause to worry about the approaching deadline, I have just settled down to watch one of the most uncomfortable films ever made.

Titled *Peeping Tom* and directed by Michael Powell, the film met with such a poor reception on its release in 1960 (the *Observer* critic was "disgusted," *Tribune*'s remedy was "to shovel it up and flush it swiftly down the nearest sewer") that it lay in the memory banks of a few maverick critics and film students until Martin Scorsese brought it to the world's attention at the New York Film Festival in 1979.

I'd already seen *Peeping Tom* maybe three times before. I'd digested its horror—the serial killer who films his victims as he kills them with the spiked leg of his camera . . . and, it is later revealed, reflects their own fear back at them via a mirror attached to his equipment. I was also familiar enough with the film to get the most out of its underlying comic elements—like that gag about being a photographer from the *Observer*. The last thing on the menu was surprise.

The credits roll. An eye blinks on screen and the first scene is unveiled. It is . . . the cover of *The Rise and Fall of Ziggy Stardust and the Spiders from Mars*. The film's protagonist, Mark Lewis, approaches a prostitute, who is standing by a wall in a dimly lit street. Boxed debris fills the foreground, right-side. Up ahead, sandwiched between and above the darkened buildings, is the night sky.

So the film has another fan, albeit one who, to my knowledge, has never declared his interest. This discovery provides a vital clue in the decoding of *Ziggy Stardust,* but one that, to my relief, justifies rather than undermines the content of this book. Driven by powerful themes of psychological breakdown and the relationship between the auteur and his audience, not to mention its neon-lit voyeurism, *Peeping Tom* is surely the missing link that binds together the important elements in the construction of Bowie's most complete achievement. Has his cover finally been blown?

THE REVIEWS

Rolling Stone
20 JULY 1972
BY RICHARD CROMELIN

Upon the release of David Bowie's most thematically ambitious, musically coherent album to date, the record on which he unites the major strengths of his previous work and comfortably reconciles himself to some apparently inevitable problems, we should all say a brief prayer that his fortunes are not made to rise and fall with the fate of the "drag-rock" syndrome—that thing that's manifesting itself in the self-conscious quest for decadence which is all the rage at the moment in trendy Hollywood, in Alice Cooper's presentation, and, way down in the pits, in such grotesqueries as Queen, Nick St. Nicholas' trio of feathered, sequined Barbie dolls. And which is bound to get worse.

For although Lady Stardust himself has probably had more to do with androgyny's current fashionableness in rock than any other individual, he has never made his sexuality anything more than a completely natural and integral part of his public self, refusing to lower it to the level of gimmick but never excluding it from his image and craft. To do either would involve an artistically fatal degree of compromise.

Which is not to say that he hasn't had a great time with it. Flamboyance and outrageousness are inseparable from that campy image of his, both in the Bacall and Garbo stages and in his new butch, street-crawler appearance that has him looking like something out of the darker pages of "City of Night." It's all tied up with the one aspect of David Bowie that sets him apart from both the exploiters of transvestisism and writer/performers of comparable talent—his theatricality.

The news here is that he's managed to get that sensibility down on vinyl, not with an attempt at pseudo-visualism (which, as Mr Cooper has

Bowie, "Midnight Special" filming, Autumn 1973 ©1973, 1996 MICK ROCK, COURTESY OF STAR FILE

117

shown, just doesn't cut it), but through employment of broadly mannered styles and deliveries, a boggling variety of vocal nuances that provide the program with the necessary depth, a verbal acumen that is now more economic and no longer clouded by storms of psychotic, frenzied music, and, finally, a thorough command of the elements of rock & roll. It emerges as a series of concise vignettes designed strictly for the ear.

Side two is the soul of the album, a kind of psychological equivalent of "Lola vs. Powerman" that delves deep into a matter close to David's heart: what's it all about to be a rock & roll star? It begins with the slow, fluid "Lady Stardust," a song in which currents of frustration and triumph merge in an overriding desolation. For though "He was alright, the band was altogether" [sic], still "People stared at the makeup on his face / Laughed at his long black hair, his animal grace." The pervading bitter-sweet melancholy that wells out of the contradictions and that Bowie beautifully captures with one of the album's more direct vocals conjures the picture of a painted harlequin under the spotlight of a deserted the-ater in the darkest hour of the night.

"Star" springs along handsomely as he confidently tells us that "I could make it all worthwhile as a rock & roll star." Here Bowie outlines the dazzling side of the coin: "so inviting—so enticing to play the part." His singing is a delight, full of mocking intonations and backed way down in the mix with excessive, marvelously designed "Ooooohh la la la"'s and such that they are both a joy to listen to and part of the parodic under-current that runs through the entire album.

"Hang On to Yourself" is both a kind of warning and an irresistible erotic rocker (especially the hand-clapping chorus), and apparently Bowie has decided that since he just can't avoid cramming too many syl-lables into his lines, he'll simply master the rapid-fire, tongue-twisting phrasing that his failing requires. *Ziggy Stardust* has a faint ring of *The Man Who Sold The World* to it—stately, measured, fuzzily electric. A tale of intragroup jealousies, it features some of Bowie's more adventurous imagery, some of which really is the nazz: "So we bitched about his fans and should we crush his sweet hands?"

David Bowie's supreme moment as a rock & roller is "Suffragette City," a relentless, spirited Velvet Underground–styled rush of chomping guitars. When that second layer of guitar roars in on the second verse you're bound to be a goner, and that priceless little break at the end—a sudden cut to silence from a mighty crescendo, Bowie's voice oozing out as a brittle, charged "Ooooohh Wham Bam Thank You Ma'am!" followed hard by two raspy guitar bursts that suck you back into the surging meat of the chorus—will surely make your tum do somersaults. And as for our Star, well, now "There's only room for one and here she comes, here she comes."

But the price of playing the part must be paid, and we're precipitously tumbled into the quietly terrifying despair of "Rock & Roll Suicide." The broken singer drones: "Time takes a cigarette, puts it in your mouth / Then you pull on your finger, then another finger, then your cigarette." But there is a way out of the bleakness, and it is realized with Bowie's Lennon-like scream: "You're not alone, gimme your hands / You're wonderful, gimme your hands." It rolls on to a tumultous, impassioned climax, and though the mood is not exactly sunny, a desperate, possessed optimism asserts itself as genuine, and a new point from which to climb is firmly established.

Side one is certainly less challenging, but no less enjoyable from a musical standpoint. Bowie's favorite themes—Mortality ("Five Years," "Soul Love"), the necessity of reconciling oneself to Pain (those two and "It Ain't Easy"), the New Order vs. the Old in sci-fi garments ("Starman")—are presented with a consistency, a confidence, and a strength in both style and technique that were never fully realized in the lashing *The Man Who Sold The World* or the uneven and too often stringy "Hunky Dory."

Bowie initiates "Moonage Daydream" on side one with a riveting bellow of "I'm an alligator" that's delightful in itself but which also has a lot to do with what "Rise And Fall . . ." is all about. Because in it there's the perfect touch of self-mockery, a lusty but forlorn bravado that is the first hint of the central duality and of the rather spine-tingling questions that rise from it: Just how big and tough is your rock & roll star? How much of him is bluff and how much inside is very frightened and helpless? And is this what comes of our happily dubbing someone as "bigger than life"?

David Bowie has pulled off his complex task with consummate style, with some great rock & roll (the Spiders are Mick Ronson on guitar and piano, Mick Woodmansey on drums and Trevor Bolder on bass; they're good), with all the wit and passion required to give it sufficient dimension and with a deep sense of humanity that regularly emerges from behind the Star facade. The important thing is that despite the formidable nature of the undertaking, he hasn't sacrificed a bit of entertainment value for the sake of message.

I'd give it at least a 99.

Melody Maker
1 JULY 1972
BY MICHAEL WATTS

The cover of Bowie's new album has a picture of him in a telephone booth looking every inch the stylish poseur. Style and content have now become inextricably tangled in Bowie's case. Campness has become built-in to his public persona. I mean that, however, in a far from derogatory sense. The main preoccupation of David's work is not directly with gay sexuality, though that element is there, as with a flourishing theatricality and dramatic sense. On *Ziggy Stardust* this is apparent even with a song like "Five Years." Ostensibly about the death of the world, Bowie turns it into a "performance" by virtue of his gift for artful mannerism and by creating a convincing mise-en-scène (a cop kneels at the feet of a priest and a soldier is run over by a car after it is announced on the news that the earth has five years left). It would also go some way towards explaining why this album has such a conceptual-sounding title. There is no well-defined story line, as there is in "Tommy," say, but there are odd songs and references to the business of being a pop star that overall add up to a strong sense of biographical drama. On one track, "Star," he sings about playing "the wild mutation of a rock and roll star." ("I'd send my photograph to my honey and I'd c'mon like a regular superstar.") Then "Ziggy Stardust," the title track, is about a guitar superhero who "took it all too far." ("Making love with his ego Ziggy sucked up into his mind.") The final track is simply called "Rock 'n' Roll Suicide," it speaks for itself. In the space of three songs he thus suggests the ascent and decline of a big rock figure, but leaves the listener to fill in his own details, and in the process he's also referring obliquely to his own role as a rock star and sending it up. There are many layers to Bowie the artist, but he has this uncanny knack of turning a whole album or stage performance into a torch song. *Ziggy Stardust* is a little less instantly appealing than *Hunky Dory,* basically because that album was written with the intention of being commercial. This one rocks more, though, and the paradox is that it will be much more commercially successful than the last, because Bowie's bid for stardom is accelerating at lightning speed.

Phonograph Record
August 1972
By Jim Bickhart

Since jumping from Mercury to RCA, David Bowie has added the decipherable touch to his recordings which they needed to reach more than the esoteric crew of rock critics his two Mercury albums were embraced by. Consequently, the newer records, first *Hunky Dory* and now *Ziggy Stardust,* are selling, and Bowie is ripping up English audiences with a stage show calculated to embarrass everyone from T. Rex to the Cockettes.

Five years ago, Bowie was making typically English rock and roll story records, his image late '60s flash mod flower child. Then he moved on to poetry and art rock, going through a semi-acoustic phase and an odd hit record called "Space Oddity," which reflected both his interests in rebelliousness and intergalactic matters. Next came some very electric, at times almost heavy-metal psychotic commentary by way of a powerful album called "The Man Who Sold The World."

Ziggy Stardust, the outgrowth of Bowie's new openness, is a self-contained rock and roll album about rock and roll. Bowie's band, guitarist Mick Ronson, bassist [*sic*] Mick Woodmansey and drummer [*sic*] Trevor Bolder team with the singer/guitarist to both perform and play the roles depicted in the album's songs; to a limited extent, they are Ziggy Stardust and the Spiders from Mars. And most certainly, they are an excellent rock band.

The songs, beginning with the doom-portending "Five Years," create a tale in which a number of Bowie's beliefs and fantasies are placed in full view. The thread of the plot goes from the announcement of impending doom through the uncontrollability of love ("Soul Love") to a major turning point, "Moonage Daydream," where Ziggy, whoever he is before he actually becomes Ziggy, is zapped by a combination of religion (first invoked at the end of "Soul Love"), romance, rock and roll and bisexuality. Symbolically, it is perhaps the album's most important number.

From this point, the new rock and roll idol, ostensibly an invader from space (though it is really the space in someone's active imagination), begins making himself public. "Starman" presents his arrival on earth both as a religious phenomenon and as a religious occurrence. A stylised rendition of Ron Davies' "It Ain't Easy" takes Ziggy on a sexual tangent to finish side one.

Side two is more directly devoted to the rise and fall of Ziggy and the Spiders. "Lady Stardust" says, in no uncertain terms, that this rock star appeals sexually to Everyone in the audience, just as is actually the case with most superstars (Bowie, though, has a way of not mincing his words). "Star" offers the singer's motivations for seeking fame, and "Hang On To Yourself" describes the position of the band as they begin to discover the nature of their appeal and what they must do to make it big. *Ziggy Stardust* compresses, in rock ballad form, the basic story of the band's fling with stardom. The final pair of numbers, the ballsy "Suffragette City" and "Rock And Roll Suicide" are a bit anti-climactic in content. "Suffragette" is pure lust and out of sequence (it would seem more comfortable if heard before the idea of Ziggy's downfall is introduced), though it is the album's classic rocker in the Rolling Stones sense. "Suicide" is a symbolic referent for the idea of what the forgotten idol does after the fall.

David Bowie, on the strength of his five albums, is certainly one of the most distinctive personalities in rock, and that alone is enough to make his very listenable records a bit extraordinary. Even if some of his ideas don't quite work out, his talent for strong conception and sound execution is undeniable. Should he become a star of the *Ziggy Stardust* magnitude, he will deserve it, and hopefully his daydreams won't be forced to turn to suicide when it's all over.

New Musical Express
3 JUNE 1972
BY JAMES JOHNSON

With most of his material either dealing with the flashier style of city living or looking far into the future, Bowie must rate as our most futuristic songwriter. Sometimes what he sees is just a little scary, and perhaps there's a bit more pessimism here than on previous releases, but they're still fine songs.

Like the first track, "Five Years," about the imminent death of a decaying world, is a real downer to start with, but Bowie brings a new approach to the rather overworked theme.

Certainly all the tracks, written by Bowie with the exception of Ron Davies's "It Ain't Easy," are never less than entertaining. "Soul Love" features some withdrawn sax from Mick Ronson. "Ziggy Stardust" deals with the destruction of a rock star, while "Hang On to Yourself" is a real little sexual gem. Also included is Bowie's current single, "Starman."

Mick Ronson (bass and sax) [*sic*], Trevor Bolder (bass) and Mick Woodmansey (drums) handle the backing all through.

Of course there's nothing Bowie would like more than to be a glittery super-star, and it could still come to pass. By now everybody ought to know he's tremendous and this latest chunk of fantasy can only enhance his reputation further.

Bowie, between Mick Ronson's legs, UK Summer tour, 1973
©1973, 1996 MICK ROCK, COURTESY OF STAR FILE

CHRONOLOGY

February

Bowie outlines plans for his *Ziggy Stardust* concept to celebrity DJ Rodney Bingenheimer and RCA executive Tom Ayers while on a promotional tour of the States publicizing *The Man Who Sold the World.*

April 1

John Mendelsohn writes the first major piece on Bowie in the United States for *Rolling Stone* magazine. Titled "David Bowie: Pantomime Rock?" it outlines the singer's performance-as-spectacle manifesto.

June 5

At a recording for BBC Radio 1's "The Sunday Show," emcee John Peel announces that the first single by Arnold Corns is called "Moonage Daydream." The show, which features the public debut of Bowie backed by future Spiders Mick Ronson and Mick "Woody" Woodmansey (with Tony Visconti on bass), is broadcast on 20 June.

September 8

Iggy Pop signs a management deal with Tony Defries.

September 9

Bowie and Defries sign a deal with RCA Records in New York for the relatively modest fee of $37,500 per album. In the evening, they meet Lou Reed and Iggy Pop at an RCA dinner party held at Max's Kansas City.

November

During the first two weeks of the month, "Star,""Hang On to Yourself," "Sweet Head," "Moonage Daydream," "Soul Love," and "Lady Stardust" are recorded at Trident Studios, London. Other songs begun but never finished include "It's Gonna Rain," "Shadow Man," "Only One Paper Left," and "Looking for a Friend."

December 15

A provisional master tape for the *Ziggy Stardust* album is made.
Side one: *Five Years / Soul Love / Moonage Daydream / Round and Round (Berry) / Port Of Amsterdam (Brel)*
Side two: *Hang On to Yourself / Ziggy Stardust / Velvet Goldmine / Holy Holy / Star / Lady Stardust*

1972

January

During the middle of the month, the final *Ziggy Stardust* songs, "Starman," "Rock 'n' Roll Suicide," and "Suffragette City," are taped.

22

Bowie, billed as "rock's swishiest outrage," appears on the cover of *Melody Maker*. Michael Watts's "Oh You Pretty Thing" feature reports Bowie as saying "I'm gay, and always have been, even when I was David Jones." It is later known as his "I'm Gay" confession piece.

28

A session for Radio 1's "Sounds of the '70s" show, hosted by John Peel, previews two *Ziggy Stardust* songs, "Hang On to Yourself" and "Ziggy Stardust." Also performed: "Queen Bitch" and "Waiting for the Man" (Reed). "Lady Stardust," taped at the same session, is broadcast on 3 March.

29

Dry run for the first Ziggy tour at Aylesbury Friars. Bowie unveils his new Ziggy image, wearing a patterned two-piece outfit and sporting newly shorn orange hair.

February 2

A second *Ziggy Stardust* master tape still includes "Round and Round." It will later be replaced by "Starman."

7

More *Ziggy Stardust* material is aired on a specially recorded session (taped on 18 January) for Radio 1, this time on Bob Harris's "Sounds of the '70s" show: Ziggy Stardust / Hang On to Yourself / Five Years / Queen Bitch. "Waiting for the Man" (Reed) has also been recorded, but is not broadcast. The program also includes an interview with Bowie.

8

The national unveiling of Bowie's new look takes place on BBC-TV's *The Old Grey Whistle Test.* He performs two songs from the *Hunky Dory* album, "Queen Bitch" and "Oh! You Pretty Things" and previews "Five Years."

10

The first of two U.K. tours begins at the Toby Jug, Tolworth, in Surrey.

April 14

The "Starman" 45 is released.

May

"Starman" is released in the United States.

6

Several journalists are invited to a show at Kingston Polytechnic. The music press reports that a new album and tour are on the way.

23

More prepublicity, courtesy of BBC's Radio 1, comes in the form of "Hang On to Yourself," "Ziggy Stardust," "Suffragette City," and "White Light/White Heat" (Reed), taped for John Peel's "Top Gear" show. Also recorded, but not broadcast: "Moonage Daydream."

June

"John, I'm Only Dancing" is recorded at Trident Studios in London.

5–9	A weeklong Bowie promotion on the prime-time Johnny Walker show, which airs "Oh! You Pretty Things," "Space Oddity," "Changes," and "Starman." These versions (taped on 22 May) include guitar and vocal overdubs, and are marginally different than the studio recordings. The publicity helps break "Starman."
6	*The Rise and Fall of Ziggy Stardust and the Spiders from Mars* is released in the United Kingdom.
10	It is reported that Bowie is producing the new Mott the Hoople album and will produce the new Lou Reed LP in August.
17	Mick Rock snaps the infamous "fellatio" photo at the Oxford Town Hall concert during "Suffragette City." It is quickly circulated to the press by RCA.
19	BBC Radio broadcasts "Rock 'n' Roll Suicide," "Lady Stardust," "Andy Warhol," and "White Light/White Heat" (Reed). The session, taped on 23 May and aired on Bob Harris's Radio 1 show, is Bowie's last for the BBC for almost 20 years. It is repeated on 25 July, this time with an extra track, "Moonage Daydream."
30	Defries forms his management company, Mainman, in a deal that gives him control of both Bowie and the master tapes for ten years.
July 1	*The Rise and Fall of Ziggy Stardust and the Spiders from Mars* debuts on the *Melody Maker* chart at number 19, a position it shares with another new entry, *Rory Gallagher Live in Europe.*
8	At a benefit show at the Festival Hall, London, Bowie invites Lou Reed on stage. The pair perform three songs from the Velvet Underground canon. Meanwhile, a

full-page ad based on the "fellatio" shot appears in the U.K. press.

14

Lou Reed makes his U.K. debut at the King's Cross Cinema, London.

15

A group of American journalists are flown over to see Bowie perform at Aylesbury Friars. Afterward, they attend a midnight show by Iggy Pop at the King's Cross Cinema, London.
The same day, a *Melody Maker* review of the Festival Hall show, written by Ray Coleman, declares "A Star Is Born." "Starman" makes a belated entrance on the singles chart.

August 19

A new show is unveiled at the Rainbow, complete with moving images, a multilevel stage, and a dance troupe. Earlier that day, a promotional video for "John, I'm Only Dancing" is shot at the venue by Mick Rock. *Melody Maker* carries an exclusive two-page interview, billed as "The Rise and Rise of Ziggy Stardust." A full-page ad in the same issue proclaims that "David Bowie Is Ziggy Stardust Live at the Rainbow."

20

A second night at the Rainbow will be Bowie's last U.K. appearance until the autumn. Reviewing the show, Chris Welch writes: "By God, it has brought a little glamour into all our lives, and Amen to that."

September 2

Bowie returns to play the first of two nights opening the Manchester Hardrock.

22

The first American tour opens in Cleveland, Ohio.

28

Bowie plays the prestigious Carnegie Hall in New York. Press and glitterati turn out in force. Reporting back to the United Kingdom, journalist Roy Hollingworth claims he overhears an audience member declaring, "The '60s are over, well and truly over."

October	Bowie records his own version of "All the Young Dudes" in New York. It is later mixed by Bowie and Ken Scott back at Trident.
6	"The Jean Genie" is recorded.
7	"The Jean Genie" is debuted on stage in Chicago.
20	It is reported that RCA has recorded three shows on the American tour for a live album to be released in time for Christmas. That evening, Bowie's performance at the Santa Monica Civic Auditorium is broadcast on American radio. This forms the basis of two of the best-selling bootlegs ever.
November	Lou Reed's *Transformer,* produced by David Bowie and Mick Ronson, is released.
9	Tony Defries tells *Rolling Stone,* "[Bowie's] very much a '70s artist . . . he is one person of many facets and many talents who can be and will be an industry of his own."
11	Advertisements appear for the reissues of "Space Oddity" and *The Man Who Sold the World* under the slogan, "Make Room for 2 Bowie Albums."
17	"Drive-In Saturday" is debuted on stage in Miami.
29	Bowie travels to Philadelphia to introduce Mott the Hoople on stage. He joins the group for a version of "All the Young Dudes."
December	Work begins in New York on sessions for *Aladdin Sane.*
9	U.K. dates in December and January are announced with advertisements proclaiming "Bowie's Back!"

16

The same advertising theme is continued the following week: "RCA Welcomes Bowie Back from his triumphant tour of the U.S."

23

Another *Melody Maker* cover proclaims Bowie as "THE main man of 1972, just as we predicted when we front-paged him back in January." Bowie dominates the issue: *The Rise and Fall of Ziggy Stardust and the Spiders from Mars* is the critics' choice for pop album of the year; a two-page ad carries a seasonal message, "David Bowie and the Spiders wish everyone a Happy Christmas," and suggests that those going to the Rainbow show bring a toy to be donated to a children's charity; in a report from a New York press conference, Bowie describes the United States as having "the aura of being conditioned and built by McDonald's and Woolworth's."

24

Bowie makes a triumphant U.K. return at the Rainbow. The show opens with a version of the Stones' "Let's Spend the Night Together," as it would at concerts in 1973.

January

Bowie's 1969 album, now retitled *Space Oddity,* is issued in the States.
U.K. tour begins. The band is enlarged to include Geoff McCormack (vocals, percussion), Ken Fordham (sax), Mike Garson (piano, Mellotron), John "Hutch" Hutchinson (rhythm guitar, vocals), and Brian Wilshaw (sax, flute).
The "sax" version of "John, I'm Only Dancing" is recorded.

6

A *Melody Maker* reader takes issue with the paper's choice of *Ziggy Stardust* as album of the year. "Just what have you been attracted by?" complains Steve Ralphs from Somerset. "Bowie's introverted 'poetry' which has as much relevance to his substandard dustbin rock as his 'camp aura' has to Frankenstein? If this is the best album of the year, then what are we to expect in 1973—*Shirley Temple's Greatest Hits?* God help rock."

13	Reports suggest that two new Bowie albums, including the promised live set, are imminent.
17	Bowie appears on the *Russell Harty Plus* television talk show. He performs "My Death" and "Drive-In Saturday."
25	The singer boards the QE2 for a world tour that will continue until late April.
February 14	Bowie collapses onstage at the Radio City Music Hall in New York.
24	A *Melody Maker* cover story is headlined "Bowie's Last Tour?" Tony Defries tells the paper that Bowie "may not make another British tour after this one for a long, long time, maybe even years, especially if he gets into films." Michael Watts meets Bowie in New York for a two-page feature titled "Stranger in a Strange Land."
March	Early in the month, Bowie spends time with Iggy Pop in Western Sound Studios, Los Angeles, mixing the tapes for *Raw Power.*
April 5	Arrives in Japan for a short tour.
21	Leaves Japan.
May	Five Bowie albums are lodged in the U.K. charts. *Aladdin Sane* debuts at number 1 and stays there for five weeks. Iggy and the Stooges' *Raw Power* is released in the United Kingdom.
12	The concert at Earls Court, London, is blighted by crowd trouble, poor visibility, and sound problems. Headlines like "What Went Wrong?" and "Bowie Fiasco" yield the first significant bad press post–*Ziggy*

Stardust. A second concert scheduled for the venue in June is canceled, and the considerably smaller Hammersmith Odeon is booked instead.

It is all smiles, though, on the front page of *Melody Maker,* which carries a picture of David and Angie. The reason? Everyone's "Bowie Mad!" Inside, Bowie tells Roy Hollingworth that he's tired of touring. "I just want to bloody well go home to Beckenham and watch the telly," he says.

June

Rock highbrows Dave Laing and Simon Frith put forward "Two Views of the Glitter Prince of Rock" in *Let It Rock* magazine. Laing insists that Bowie "has compromised with the whole manipulative process of image and stardom. . . . Take away Bowie's image and there's nothing left." Frith disagrees: "Cold and calculated, maybe, but a scarily complete vision of life in the rock culture—sensual, selfish, endless."

3

Toward the end of a concert at the Hammersmith Odeon, Bowie declares, "It's the last show that we'll ever do. Thank you." Afterward, Bowie celebrates his "retirement" with a celebrity-packed party at the Café Royal on London's Regent Street.

4

Mainman issues a statement to the press confirming that Bowie is "leaving the concert stage forever."

5

BBC's prime-time television news show, *Nationwide,* broadcasts a lengthy investigation of the Bowie phenomenon.

July

Bowie is voted the "World's Best Male Singer" in *Music Scene.*

1

Defries negotiates a lucrative new deal with RCA. Advances on albums are now $60,000, rising to $200,000 by 1976, and Bowie's royalty is raised.

14	"Is Bowie Really Quitting?" asks Roy Hollingworth in *Melody Maker.* His conclusion? "Don't worry kids, it's just tactics." According to Mick Ronson, "He'll be back. . . . We haven't even started yet. David has to keep changing."
23	There are five Bowie albums in the U.K. Top 40, including three in the Top 15.
October	*Pin Ups,* Bowie's affectionate tribute to mid-sixties British pop, is released.
18–20	Filming at the Marquee Club, London, for broadcast on American TV marks Bowie's final concert with Mick Ronson. The Ziggy era comes to a close with a performance of "Rock 'n' Roll Suicide."

DISCOGRAPHY

Starman / Suffragette City

RCA 2199; some in picture sleeve; released April 1972; No. 10

John, I'm Only Dancing / Hang On to Yourself

RCA 2263; released September 1972; No. 12
    From April 1973, A-sides featured a different "sax" version.

The Jean Genie / Ziggy Stardust

RCA 2302; released November 1972; U.K. No. 2

Drive-In Saturday / Round and Round

RCA 2352; released April 1973; No. 3; B-side features *Ziggy Stardust* outtake

Life on Mars? / The Man Who Sold the World

RCA 2316; some in picture sleeve; released June 1973; No. 3

The Rise and Fall of Ziggy Stardust and the Spiders from Mars

RCA SF 8287; with lyric inner sleeve; No. 5; June 1972
Five Years / Soul Love / Moonage Daydream / Starman / It Ain't Easy / Lady Stardust / Star / Hang On to Yourself / Ziggy Stardust / Suffragette City / Rock 'n' Roll Suicide

The Man Who Sold the World

November 1972 reissue of 1971 LP; RCA LSP 4816; No. 26

The Width of a Circle / All the Madmen / Black Country Rock / After All / Running Gun Blues / Saviour Machine / She Shook Me Cold / The Man Who Sold the World / The Supermen

Space Oddity

November 1972 reissue of 1969 LP; RCA LSP 4813; No. 17

Space Oddity / Unwashed and Somewhat Slightly Dazed / Letter to Hermione / Cygnet Committee / Janine / An Occasional Dream / Wild Eyed Boy from Freecloud / God Knows I'm Good / Memory of a Free Festival

Aladdin Sane

April 1973; RCA RS 1001; gatefold sleeve & lyric inner sleeve; No. 1

Watch that Man / Aladdin Sane / Drive-In Saturday / Panic in Detroit / Cracked Actor / Time / The Prettiest Star / Let's Spend the Night Together / The Jean Genie / Lady Grinning Soul

The World of David Bowie

April 1973 reissue of 1970 compilation in new "Ziggy" sleeve; Decca SPA 58

Uncle Arthur / Love You till Tuesday / There Is a Happy Land / Little Bombardier / Sell Me a Coat / The London Boys / Karma Man / Rubber Band / Let Me Sleep Beside You / Come and Buy My Toys / She's Got Medals / In the Heat of the Morning / When I Live My Dream

---

U.S. Singles

Starman / Suffragette City

RCA 74–0719; May 1972; in picture sleeve

The Jean Genie / Hang On to Yourself

RCA 74–0838; November 1972; in picture sleeve; No. 71

Space Oddity / Moonage Daydream / Life on Mars? / It Ain't Easy

RCA EP 45103; December 1972; in picture sleeve; No. 15

Space Oddity / The Man Who Sold the World

RCA 74–0876; January 1973; in picture sleeve

Time / The Prettiest Star

RCA APBO 0007; April 1973; in picture sleeve

Let's Spend the Night Together / Lady Grinning Soul

RCA APBO 0028; June 1973; in picture sleeve

The Rise and Fall of Ziggy Stardust and the Spiders from Mars

RCA LSP 4702; June 1972; with lyric inner sleeve

Space Oddity

RCA LSP 4813; September 1972; No. 16

The Man Who Sold the World

RCA LSP 4816; September 1972

Aladdin Sane

RCA AFL1 4852; April 1973; gatefold sleeve & lyric inner sleeve; No. 17

Reissues of non-RCA material have not been included except for those that charted.

In the U.K., the album was issued at budget price in January 1981 (RCA International INTS 5063), where it reentered the chart, reaching number 33. Three years later, in March 1984, it reappeared in picture disc form (RCA BOPIC 3), and it made its first appearance on CD in 1985 (RCA PD 84702).

In 1990, an enlarged CD/vinyl edition (EMI CDP 0777/EMC 3577; also on Rykodisc in the U.S., where the LP was pressed on clear virgin vinyl), containing "John, I'm Only Dancing" and "Velvet Goldmine," three previously unissued demos of "Sweet Head," "Ziggy Stardust," and "Lady Stardust," plus enhanced artwork, was issued as part of a major retrospective campaign. Ryko also pressed a promo edition containing both CD and vinyl, inviting reviewers to compare the difference. This came with several inserts.

A half-speed mastered vinyl edition (Mobile Fidelity MFSL 1-064) is available on the U.S. market, while in 1997, EMI in the U.K. pressed a limited edition on vinyl (7243 8 55666 1 5) as part of its EMI "100 Classic Albums" promotion.

Related
Singles

Moonage Daydream / Hang On to Yourself

as Arnold Corns, May 1971; B&C CB 149

This single, credited to the pseudonymous Arnold Corns, features early working versions of material recorded later in the year for the *Ziggy Stardust* album.

Sorrow / Amsterdam

October 1973; U.K.: RCA 2424; No. 3/U.S.: APBO 0160

The B-side, a Jacques Brel number, was a regular fixture of Ziggy shows.

Rock 'n' Roll Suicide / Quicksand

April 1974; U.K./U.S.: RCA LPBO 5021; U.K. No. 22

Almost two years after the album, Ziggy bowed out one more time. It was his least successful U.K. 45 since "Changes" had failed to chart early in 1972.

Space Oddity / Changes / Velvet Goldmine

RCA 2593; September 1975; some in picture sleeve; U.K. No. 1

A first outing for *Ziggy Stardust* outtake "Velvet Goldmine."

Suffragette City / Stay

U.K.: RCA 2726; July 1976; some in picture sleeve

A certain Top 10 hit had it been issued in 1972, "Suffragette City" failed miserably on the back of Bowie's 1976 European tour.

John, I'm Only Dancing (Again) (1975) / John, I'm Only Dancing (1972)

RCA BOW 4; December 1979; picture sleeve; U.K. No. 12

Also on twelve-inch (BOW 12–4).

Related
Albums

Ziggy Stardust: The Motion Picture

October 1983; 2-LP; U.K.: RCA PL 84862; No. 17; also on CD: EMI 0777, 1992

Hang On to Yourself / Ziggy Stardust / Watch That Man / Wild Eyed Boy from Freecloud—All The Young Dudes—Oh! You Pretty Things! [medley] / Moonage Daydream / Space Oddity/ My Death / Cracked Actor / Time / The Width of a Circle / Changes / Let's Spend the Night Together / Suffragette City / White Light-White Heat / Rock 'n' Roll Suicide

The soundtrack to D. A. Pennebaker's documentary film of the July 1973 Hammersmith Odeon concert.

Sound + Vision

November 1989; 3-CD+CDV EP/6-LP box set; U.S.: Rykodisc RCD/RALP 0120/21/22–2

Space Oddity [demo] / Wild Eyed Boy from Freecloud / The Prettiest Star / London Bye Ta-Ta / Black Country Rock / The Man Who Sold the World / The Bewlay Brothers / Changes / Round and Round / Moonage Daydream / John, I'm Only Dancing / Drive-In Saturday / Panic in Detroit / Ziggy Stardust [live] / White Light-White Heat [live] / Rock 'n' Roll Suicide [live] / Anyway, Anyhow, Anywhere / Sorrow / Don't Bring Me Down / 1984-Dodo / Big Brother / Rebel Rebel / Suffragette City [live] / Watch That Man [live] / Cracked Actor [live] / Young Americans / Fascination / After Today / It's Hard to Be a Saint in the City / TVC15 / Wild Is the Wind / Sound and Vision / Be My Wife / Speed of Life / Helden / Joe the Lion / Sons of the Silent Age / Staton to Station [live] / Warszawa [live] / Breaking Glass [live] / Red Sails / Look Back in Anger / Boys Keep Swinging / Up the Hill Backwards / Kingdom Come / Ashes to Ashes; plus CDV: John, I'm Only Dancing [live] / Changes [live] / The Supermen [live] / Ashes to Ashes

This is probably the best entree into Bowie's career yet compiled (though it is not a best of), and it is excellently packaged, too. The bonus CDV includes three tracks recorded live at the Boston Music Hall on 1 October 1972: "John I'm Only Dancing," "Changes," and "The Supermen." "Round and Round" and the 1973 version of "John, I'm Only Dancing" are other notable *Ziggy Stardust*–era inclusions.

Santa Monica '72

April 1994; U.K.: Trident/Golden Years GY 002; No. 74/U.S.: Griffin GCD-392-2

Intro / Hang On to Yourself / Ziggy Stardust / Changes / The Supermen / Life on Mars? / Five Years / Space Oddity / Andy Warhol / My Death / The Width of a Circle / Queen Bitch / Moonage Daydream / John, I'm Only

Dancing / Waiting for the Man / The Jean Genie / Suffragette City / Rock 'n' Roll Suicide

This was an official release, issued in conjunction with Mainman, of the original Santa Monica bootleg. Griffin also released an edition of 250 in a wooden box and a concert box pressing of 1,000.

Rarestonebowie

June 1995; U.K.: Trident / Golden Years GY 014
All the Young Dudes / Queen Bitch / Sound and Vision / Time / Be My Wife / Footstompin' / Ziggy Stardust / My Death / I Feel Free

A nine-track collection of never-before-issued rarities dating from 1972 to 1978, this included Bowie's original studio version of "All the Young Dudes," taped in 1973, and live versions of two covers, Cream's "I Feel Free" (Kingston Polytechnic, 1972) and Jacques Brel's "My Death" (Carnegie Hall, 1972).

BBC Sessions 1969–1972

promo-only sampler CD, 1996; NMC NMCD 0072
Hang On to Yourself / Ziggy Stardust / Space Oddity / Andy Warhol / Waiting for the Man / Interview with Brian Matthew / Let Me Sleep Beside You

NMC planned to release three volumes of Bowie's BBC recordings, and pressed a limited number of these six-track samplers in anticipation of the launch. *Ziggy Stardust*–era recordings included "Hang On to Yourself" (broadcast 28 January 1972), "Ziggy Stardust" (23 May 1972) and "Space Oddity" (5–9 June 1972). The disc also included "Andy Warhol" (4 October 1971), "Waiting for the Man" (6 April 1970), and "Let Me Sleep Beside You" (26 October 1969), plus an interview with deejay Brian Matthew recorded in 1969.

Notable
Bootlegs

THE ZIGGY SHOWS

Kingston Polytechnic Volume 1

no number
Hang On to Yourself / Ziggy Stardust / Supermen / Queen Bitch / Song For Bob Dylan / Changes / Starman / Five Years / Space Oddity / Andy Warhol / Amsterdam

Recorded live at Kingston Polytechnic 6 May 1972.

Kingston Polytechnic Volume 2

no number

I Feel Free / Moonage Daydream / White Light-White Heat / I Got to Get a Job / Suffragette City / Rock 'n' Roll Suicide / Waiting for the Man

     Recorded live at Kingston Polytechnic 6 May 1972.

Soul Asylum

BLY 003/4, CD

Hang On to Yourself / Ziggy Stardust / Changes / Soul Love / John, I'm Only Dancing / Drive-In Saturday / Five Years / Space Oddity / My Death / The Supermen / Aladdin Sane / Panic in Detroit / Moonage Daydream / The Width of a Circle / Time / Let's Spend the Night Together / Watch That Man / Suffragette City / Rock 'n' Roll Suicide / Queen Bitch* / Song for Bob Dylan* / Changes* / Starman* / Amsterdam* / I Feel Free* / White Light-White Heat* / I Got to Get a Job* / John, I'm Only Dancing** / John, I'm Only Dancing*** / The Jean Genie****

     Recorded live at Radio City Music Hall, New York, 15 February 1973, except for items marked * taped at Kingston Polytechnic, 6 May 1972, ** from the "Russell Harty Show," January 1973, *** recorded at the "Young Americans" sessions, and **** recorded at Radio City Music Hall, 14 February 1973.

The All American Bowie

TMOQ 71074

My Death / Aladdin Sane / Five Years / The Width of a Circle / Ziggy Stardust / Changes / Panic in Detroit / Time / Suffragette City

     Recorded live at the Long Beach Arena, Long Beach, California, 10 March 1973.

Who'll Love Aladdin Sain in Tokyo

Silver & Americard SALP 1973

Hang On to Yourself / Ziggy Stardust / Changes / Moonage Daydream / Panic in Detroit / Aladdin Sane / The Jean Genie / Time / Rock 'n' Roll Suicide / This Boy

     Recorded live at the Shinjuku Kosenenkin Kaikan, Tokyo, Japan, on 8 April 1973, except for "This Boy," taped at Aylesbury Friars on 15 July 1972.

Ziggy in Japan

Duck Pro. DW 31387

Hang On to Yourself / Ziggy Stardust / Changes / Moonage Daydream / John, I'm Only Dancing / Watch That Man / The Width of a Circle / Space Oddity / The Jean Genie

Recorded live at the Yubinchokin Kaikan, Hiroshima, Japan, on 14 April 1973.

A Cat from London

YOU J-003, CD

Hang On to Yourself / Ziggy Stardust / Changes / Moonage Daydream / John, I'm Only Dancing / Watch That Man / The Jean Genie / Time / Five Years / Let's Spend the Night Together / Starman / Suffragette City / Rock 'n' Roll Suicide / Round and Round

(Possibly) recorded live at the Shibuya Kokaido, Tokyo, Japan, on 20 April 1973.

His Master's Voice

A-7374

Hang On to Yourself / Wild Eyed Boy from Freecloud—All the Young Dudes—Oh! You Pretty Things! [medley] / Moonage Daydream / Changes / Space Oddity / Time / Suffragette City / The Jean Genie—Love Me Do / Rock 'n' Roll Suicide

Recorded live at the Hammersmith Odeon on 3 July 1973, and includes "The Jean Genie—Love Me Do" medley omitted from the official motion picture soundtrack album.

Dollars in Drag

The Amazing Kornyfone

1984 / Sorrow / Everything's All Right / Space Oddity / The Supermen / Hang On to Yourself / Man in the Middle / I Can't Explain / Time / The Jean Genie / I Got You Babe

Recorded at the Marquee Club, London, on 18 and 20 October 1973, except for "The Supermen" (from the "Glastonbury Fayre" album) and "Man in the Middle" and "Hang On to Yourself" (from the Arnold Corns single).

I have not mentioned the many variations of the Santa Monica show, because it has now been made available officially.

MISCELLANEOUS

At the Beeb

Archive Pro. AP 89004

White Light-White Heat / Let Me Sleep Beside You / Unwashed and Somewhat Slightly Dazed / Wild Eyed Boy from Freecloud / Bombers / Looking for a Friend / Almost Grown / Kooks / The Supermen / Ziggy Stardust / Five Years / Starman / Rock 'n' Roll Suicide / Hang On to Yourself / Waiting for the Man

    Recorded for BBC Radio, 1969–1972.

A Crash Course for the Ravers

no number

Queen Bitch / Bombers / The Supermen / Looking for a Friend / Almost Grown / Kooks / Song for Bob Dylan / Andy Warhol / It Ain't Easy / Changes / Andy Warhol / The Supermen / Ziggy Stardust / Five Years / Waiting for the Man / White Light-White Heat / Rock 'n' Roll Suicide / Starman / Drive-In Saturday / Janine

    Recorded for BBC Radio except "Starman" from Top of the Pops (1972) and "Drive-In Saturday" from the "Russell Harty Show" (1973).

Starman in Session

Silver Rarities SIRA 93

Love You till Tuesday / When I Live My Dream / The Little Bombardier / Silly Boy Blue / In the Heat of the Morning / Waiting for the Man / The Width of a Circle / Wild Eyed Boy from Freecloud / Suffragette City / Hang On to Yourself / White Light-White Heat / Moonage Daydream / Ziggy Stardust / John, I'm Only Dancing / Lady Stardust / Starman / Changes

    Recorded for BBC Radio.

Missing Links One Ziggy

ICON ONE, CD

The Supermen / Lightning Frightening / Tired of My Life / All the Madmen / Holy Holy / How Lucky You Are / Andy Warhol (intro) / Looking for a Friend / Man in the Middle / The Shadow Man / Looking for a Friend / Waiting for the Man / Oh! You Pretty Things / Queen Bitch / Five Years / White Light-White Heat / A Lad in Vain / All the Young Dudes / The Jean Genie—Love Me Do / Farewell Speech (1973)

Recorded between April 1970 and July 1973, including Hunky Dory outtakes, Arnold Corns cuts, BBC recordings, plus the genuine *Ziggy Stardust* outtake of "Shadow Man."

The Shadow Man

Past Masters PM 8901, CD

I'm Just Looking for a Friend / How Lucky You Are / Shadow Man / I've Got Lightning / Rupert the Riley / Tired of My Life

Demos from the immediate pre–*Ziggy Stardust* era.

The Forgotten Songs of David Robert Jones

SPQR5CD

That's a Promise / Silly Boy Blue / Love You till Tuesday / Over the Wall We Go / When I Live My Dream / Let Me Sleep Beside You / Karma Man / Karma Man / Threepenny Pierrot / Columbine / The Mirror / When I Live My Dream / In The Heat of the Morning / London Bye Ta-Ta / Life Is a Circus / Lover to the Dawn / Love Song / Little Toy Soldier / Waiting for the Man / Rupert the Riley / Buzz the Fuzz / Right On Mother / He Was Alright (A Song for Marc Bolan)

Oddities dating from 1966 to 1970, including an early version of "Waiting for the Man" and the Velvet Underground–inspired "Silly Boy Blue."

Ziggy on Film

Ziggy Stardust and the Spiders from Mars

November 1983; Thorn-EMI TVJ 90 21132

This is D.A. Pennebaker's grainy concert documentary of the July 3, 1973, Hammersmith Odeon show.

Bowie: The Video Collection

November 1993; PMI PM 807

Includes *Ziggy Stardust*–era promo films for "Space Oddity," "John, I'm Only Dancing," "The Jean Genie," and "Life on Mars?"

Ziggy on BBC Radio

Dates refer to day of broadcast.

20 JUNE 1971	*John Peel's Sunday Show Concert:* It Ain't Easy
28 JANUARY 1972	*Sounds of the '70s:* Hang On to Yourself / Ziggy

Stardust / Queen Bitch / Waiting for the Man / Lady Stardust *(broadcast 3 March)*

7 FEBRUARY 1972	*Sounds of the '70s:* Queen Bitch / Five Years / Hang On to Yourself / Ziggy Stardust / Waiting for the Man *(not broadcast)*
23 MAY 1972	*Top Gear:* Hang On to Yourself / Ziggy Stardust / White Light-White Heat / Suffragette City / Moonage Daydream *(broadcast 25 July)*
5–9 JUNE 1972	*Johnnie Walker Show:* Oh! You Pretty Things / Starman / Space Oddity / Changes *(only the first two were broadcast)*
19 JUNE 1972	*Sounds of the '70s:* Andy Warhol / Lady Stardust / White Light-White Heat / Rock 'n' Roll Suicide
25 JULY 1972	*Sounds of the '70s:* Moonage Daydream / White Light-White Heat / Suffragette City *(partial repeat of the 23 May 1972 session)*

Ziggy on Tour
1972

JANUARY

29	*Aylesbury, Borough Assembly Rooms*

FEBRUARY

3	*Coventry, Lanchester Arts Festival*
10	*Tolworth, Toby Jug (first night proper)*
11	*High Wycombe, Town Hall*
12	*London, Imperial College, Great Hall*
14	*Brighton, Dome*
23	*Chichester College*
24	*Wallington, Public Hall*
25	*London, Avery Hill College, Eltham*

26	*Sutton Coldfield, Belfry Hotel, Mayfair Suite*
28	*Glasgow, City Hall (canceled)*
29	*Sunderland, Locarno*

MARCH

1	*Bristol University*
4	*Portsmouth, Guildhall*
7	*Yeovil, College*
11	*Southampton, Guildhall*
14	*Bournemouth, Chelsea Village*
17	*Birmingham, Town Hall*

APRIL

20	*Harlow, Playhouse*
21	*Manchester Free Trade Hall (canceled)*
29	*High Wycombe, Town Hall*
30	*Plymouth, Guildhall*

MAY

6	*Kingston, Polytechnic*
7	*Hemel Hempstead, Pavilion*
11	*Worthing, Assembly Hall*
12	*London, Central Polytechnic*
13	*Slough, Technical College*
19	*Oxford, Polytechnic*
20	*Oxford, Polytechnic*

25	*Bournemouth, Chelsea Village*
27	*Epsom, Ebbisham Hall*

JUNE

2	*Newcastle, City Hall*
3	*Liverpool, Stadium*
4	*Preston, Guildhall*
6	*Bradford, St. George's Hall*
7	*Sheffield, City Hall*
8	*Middlesborough, Town Hall*
10	*Leicester, Polytechnic*
13	*Bristol, Colston Hall*
17	*Oxford, Town Hall*
19	*Southampton, Civic Hall*
21	*Dunstable, Civic Hall*
24	*Guildford, Civic Hall*
25	*Croydon, Greyhound*

JULY

1	*Weston-Super-Mare, Winter Gardens (canceled)*
2	*Torbay, Rainbow Pavilion*
8	*London, Royal Festival Hall*
15	*Aylesbury, Friars*
18	*Aylesbury, Friars*

19	*London, Rainbow*
20	*London, Rainbow*
27	*Bristol, Locarno Electric Village*
31	*Boscombe, Bournemouth, Starkers*

SEPTEMBER

1	*Doncaster, Top Rank*
2	*Manchester, Hard Rock*
3	*Manchester, Hard Rock*
4	*Liverpool, Top Rank*
5	*Sunderland, Top Rank*
6	*Sheffield, Top Rank*
7	*Stoke-on-Trent, Hanley Top Rank*
22	*Cleveland, Music Hall*
24	*Memphis, Ellis Auditorium*
28	*New York, Carnegie Hall*
29	*Washington, D.C., John F. Kennedy Center*

OCTOBER

1	*Boston, Music Hall*
7	*Chicago, Auditorium*
8	*Detroit, Fisher Theatre*
10	*St. Louis, Music Hall*
12	*Kansas City, Auditorium*

16	*Chicago, Auditorium (canceled)*
20	*Los Angeles, Santa Monica Civic Auditorium*
21	*Los Angeles, Santa Monica Civic Auditorium*
27	*San Francisco, Winterland Auditorium*
28	*San Francisco, Winterland Auditorium*

NOVEMBER

2	*Seattle, Paramount Theater*
11	*Dallas, Majestic Theatre*
12	*Houston, Music Hall*
14	*New Orleans, Layola University*
17	*Fort Lauderdale, Pirates' World*
20	*Nashville, Municipal Auditorium*
22	*New Orleans, Warehouse*
26	*Cleveland, Entertainment Arena*
27	*Cleveland, Entertainment Arena*
28	*Pittsburgh, Stanley Theater*
29	*Philadelphia, Tower Theater (cameo at Mott the Hoople show)*
30	*Philadelphia, Tower Theater*

DECEMBER

1	*Philadelphia, Tower Theater*
2	*Philadelphia, Tower Theater*
23	*London, Rainbow*
24	*London, Rainbow*
28	*Manchester, Hard Rock*

JANUARY

5	Glasgow, Greens Pavilion (two shows)
6	Edinburgh, Empire Theatre
7	Newcastle, City Hall
9	Preston, Guildhall

FEBRUARY

14	New York, Radio City Music Hall
15	New York, Radio City Music Hall
16	Philadelphia, Tower Theater
17	Philadelphia, Tower Theater
18	Philadelphia, Tower Theater
19	Philadelphia, Tower Theater
20	Philadelphia, Tower Theater
23	Nashville, War Memorial Theater
26	Memphis, Ellis Auditorium
27	Memphis, Ellis Auditorium

MARCH

1	Detroit, Masonic Temple Auditorium
3	Chicago, Aragon Ballroom
10	Los Angeles, Long Beach Arena
11	Los Angeles, Hollywood Palladium

APRIL

| 8 | Tokyo, Shinjuku Koseinenkin Kaikan |
| 10 | Tokyo, Shinjuku Koseinenkin Kaikan |

BIBLIOGRAPHY

Bangs, Lester. *Psychotic Reactions and Carburetor Dung.* London: Heinemann, 1988.

Bowie, Angie. *Backstage Passes.* London: Orion, 1993.

Bruce, Michael. *No More Mr Nice Guy: The Inside Story of the Alice Cooper Group.* London: SAF Publishing, 1996.

Chambers, Iain. *Urban Rhythms.* London: Macmillan, 1985.

Cohn, Nik. *I Am Still the Greatest Says Johnny Angelo.* Secker & Warburg, 1967.

De La Parra, Pimm Jall. *The David Bowie Concert Tapes.* Amsterdam: Pimm Jall De La Parra, 1983.

Gillman, Peter, and Leni Gillman. *Alias David Bowie.* London: Hodder & Stoughton, 1986.

Guidal, Phil. *The Observatory.* Paris: Black Leather, 1993.

Hebdige, Dick. *Subculture: The Meaning of Style.* London: Methuen, 1979.

Juby, Kerry, ed. *In Other Words: David Bowie.* London: Omnibus, 1986.

Lynch, Kate. *David Bowie: A Rock and Roll Odyssey.* London: Proteus, 1984.

Miles, Barry, ed. *Bowie in His Own Words.* London: Omnibus, 1980.

Paytress, Mark. *Twentieth Century Boy: The Marc Bolan Story.* London: Sidgwick & Jackson, 1992.

Pitt, Kenneth. *Bowie: The Pitt Report.* London: Omnibus, 1985.

Savage, Jon. *England's Dreaming.* London: Faber & Faber, 1991.

Sontag, Susan. *Against Interpretation.* London: Vintage, 1994.

Thompson, Dave. *David Bowie: Moonage Daydream.* London: Plexus, 1987.

Thomson, Elizabeth, and David Gutman. *The Bowie Companion.* London: Macmillan, 1993.

Tremlett, George. *The David Bowie Story.* London: Futura, 1974.

I also consulted a range of magazines, most notably *Melody Maker, Music Scene, Record Collector, New Musical Express, Disc, Q,* and

Rolling Stone. Also useful were the following fanzines: *Crankin' Out!, Missing Link, Starzone,* and *Zi Duang Provence.*

BBC Radio's documentaries on Bowie, especially the six-part series in 1993, have also proven invaluable.

GENERAL INDEX

GENERAL INDEX

SONG AND ALBUM INDEX

Names in parentheses refer to performers or songwriters.

SONG AND ALBUM INDEX

ABOUT THE AUTHOR

Born in 1959 in Bournemouth, on the south coast of England, Mark Paytress is a Cultural Studies postgraduate with a thirty year-plus pedigree in rock 'n' roll studies. He is the author of *Twentieth Century Boy: The Marc Bolan Story* (Sidgwick & Jackson, 1992) and is Features Editor at *Record Collector* magazine.